FOREVER
WITH YOU

ABOUT THE AUTHOR

As a medium, lecturer, teacher, and published author, Patrick Mathews has helped countless people around the world with his gift of communicating with those who have crossed over to the other side. His acute heightened level of connection with spirit, along with his personality and heartfelt compassion, make him one of the most nationally known and sought after mediums today.

From parents, teachers, celebrities, psychologists, athletes, law enforcement agencies, individuals call upon Patrick from every walk of life. He is committed in helping people transform the quality of their lives by not only confirming the existence of their loved ones in spirit, but the continuing relationship they have with them as well!

When time permits with Patrick's busy schedule, he and his sister, Kathy Mathews, enjoy giving lectures, workshops, and demonstrations of his gift throughout the country. These events have a profound impact for those who attend.

Patrick has appeared on many national and international television and radio shows. He has also been featured in numerous magazine and newspaper articles. Patrick is the only American medium to be on the hit television shows *Most Haunted* and *Most Haunted Live*. His bestselling book *Never Say Goodbye* has helped countless readers around the world to understand and recognize their own continuing connections with loved ones in spirit. It has been published in numerous languages around the world.

Patrick Mathews

Forever With You

Inspiring Messages of Healing & Wisdom
from your Loved Ones in the Afterlife

Llewellyn Publications
Woodbury, Minnesota

First Edition
First Printing, 2012

Cover art © www.istockphoto.com
Cover design by Ellen Lawson
Editing by Connie Hill
Llewellyn is a registered trademark of Llewellyn Worldwide Ltd.

Library of Congress Cataloging-in-Publication Data

Mathews, Patrick, 1962–
  Forever with you : inspiring messages of healing & wisdom from your
loved ones in the afterlife / by Patrick Mathews.
      p.   cm.
  ISBN 978-0-7387-2766-0
1. Spiritualism. I. Title.
  BF1261.2.M38   2012
  133.9'1—dc23
2012015877

Llewellyn Publications
A Division of Llewellyn Worldwide Ltd.
2143 Wooddale Drive, Dept
Woodbury, MN 55125-2989, U.S.A.
www.llewellyn.com

Printed in the United States of America

CONTENTS

Part 3: This Life

Part4: Lighter Side of the Other Side

DEDICATION

This book is dedicated to my wonderful mother, Florence "Flossie" Mathews, and to my inspiring father, James "Snookie" Mathews.

Kathy and I have been blessed by many things in this life but having such loving, selfless, and generous parents is the greatest gift of all.

OTHER BOOKS BY PATRICK MATHEWS

Never Say Goodbye

FOREWORD

Growing up with five brothers is hard enough. Having one who is a medium and able to see ghosts at an early age was a unique and, yes, even scary experience at times. I remember during a dark summer night illuminated by the heat lightning of an approaching storm, just when we were all about to go to bed, Patrick happily alerted me to the Civil War soldier standing at my window, watching us. He then said good night like nothing had happened and went to sleep, leaving me alone, watching the seemingly empty window, looking for that night specter. I guess he thought it was funny. I should have known what was to be.

Now as adults and with his gift finely honed, I cannot get away with anything. During readings from my loved ones in spirit, they will not only convey great loving messages, but also let Patrick know that I have not been exercising enough or not finished a project that I'd started. Life with a medium is a ride; that much I can tell you. I can also tell you I would not trade it for the world.

Patrick and I have always been close and it was no surprise to anyone who knew us that we would also be working together no matter where life led us, even once we decided to go into the spiritual field. From the beginning, I have participated in and have studied many of the readings he has given. And in doing so, we both have gained vast knowledge and insight on the subjects of spirituality and the afterlife. From holding demonstrations and workshops to being interviewed on television and radio shows, we love to share with the public our years of experiences and understanding about this life and the afterlife.

If you have ever experienced a reading with Patrick then you will probably confirm what I am about to tell you. Patrick is the most compassionate, caring, humble person I know. (Believe me, if you are reading this then I won the fight with Patrick to get those compliments in.) He is truly a caring person and each one of the people he gives a reading to means the world to him. I have seen many people call themselves mediums, and even if they do have some ability, they seem to give the messages and that's it. Not caring about the person, they just do the reading and then are on to the next.

I remember Patrick and I were appearing on a television show, and while they were filming him giving a reading, a producer approached me. She seemed puzzled and asked me if this was the first time I had seen him at work. I was now the one puzzled and wanted to know why she would ask me that. She told me she had been watching me and noticed how mesmerized I looked, how intently I was watching the session. I smiled and said I had seen thousands of readings but each one was special, a gift really. Patrick was connecting with those who have passed—how amazing was that? The readings were healing the loved ones here and showing them that the connection will always continue and that love never dies. How many people get to witness that daily? I consider myself extremely blessed to be able to be a part of such an experience.

Not many people understand that Patrick not only connects with loved ones in spirit, but hears daily the sorrow and pain of the loved one receiving the reading. Many times he has heard how people do not want to go on with life and may even want to take their own life as they cannot stand the loss anymore. It takes someone so strong to absorb all of these experiences and then to show people that life does go on and so do our connections with our loved ones. Patrick is that strong person.

This book will take you inside our world and let you experience the readings, the messages, and most of all, the lessons. Patrick and I so much enjoy our in-person events such as demonstrations, workshops, and groups where sometimes maybe too much of our humor and personalities come out. It is at these events that we benefit from the personal connection we are able to have with so many who come out to see us. We learn so much from you as well. We have enjoyed traveling the world doing paranormal investigations, lectures, and television shows. We have dedicated our lives to helping others and every time we run into someone on the street or get a letter or e-mail telling us how much our work has helped, it fills our heart with such joy.

I know you will all enjoy and learn from the experiences and lessons in this book. Life and love do not have to be complicated, and through Patrick's experiences, he shows us how to take the best out of this life and continue our connections with the next.

Forgive me for getting sentimental here, but I am the luckiest sister alive. Patrick is my best friend, brother, and soul mate. He has touched many hearts, and changed many lives, mine among them.

–Kathy Mathews

Kathy Mathews is a recognized authority on spirituality, the paranormal, and the afterlife. She has participated in and studied many of the readings given by her brother, medium Patrick Mathews. With her research alongside paranormal investigations, Kathy has gained vast knowledge and insight on these subjects, and has impacted the lives of many through public speaking engagements, radio, and television. Kathy has been interviewed on many television and radio shows, and has been featured in numerous magazine and newspaper articles. She is also a published photographer.

Introduction

One of the biggest misconceptions people live with is the belief that their loved ones who have passed away into spirit are no longer a part of their lives.

I am here to tell you that not only is that not true, but it is actually quite the opposite.

Your loved ones in spirit not only continue living after their passing, but they also continue to be part of and interact with your life here as well.

Even though the majority of people in this world believe in an afterlife, many feel that their loved ones who are in spirit are far away from them, located in a place known as Heaven. Their hopes and beliefs are that their loved ones in spirit are watching over them somehow and that one day they too will be reunited with them in the afterlife.

Yes, I will admit that part of the above statement is correct and that one day we all will be joining our loved ones in Heaven … it's the "watching over" part that is totally misunderstood.

To start off, when people imagine their loved ones in spirit as "watching over them" or "watching down on them," this places a perception in the mind that Heaven then must be located somewhere up above.

And how do people get this idea of where Heaven is in the first place?

Most individuals form their ideas and opinions of what and where Heaven is from what they are taught, what is written, as well as the countless number of paintings and drawings illustrating it. All of these concepts usually will depict Heaven as being above the clouds somewhere, way beyond the sky.

And why is that?

Because if Heaven is really an actual place, then it must be beyond our physical world … or else people would be able to see it.

But the truth is, Heaven is actually not in the sky nor is it beyond the stars. In fact, Heaven really is not far away from us at all.

So then where is it?

If you're not sitting down, you may want to because you may be in for a shocker …

Heaven and those that you love in spirit are actually all around you!

As you continue reading this book, you will come to understand what I mean by this as well as how your loved ones in spirit not only watch you, but actually continue to participate in your life in ways you could never imagine!

Also in this book, I will use the term "Heaven" as well as sometimes use the term "the other side," and you may be wondering if there is a difference between the two.

The word "Heaven" instantly brings to mind a wonderful place of peace and tranquility where loved ones in spirit are conversing with the angels in the presence of God, whereas the words "the other side" feel less warm, darker, and maybe even denote a place that is not as happy. I really think that some people believe when someone crosses over into spirit, they will come across some sort of road with a sign that shows the word "Heaven" on it with an arrow pointing up, the words "the other side" with an arrow pointing straight ahead, and the word "Hell" with an arrow pointing down. Not so. When a person passes into spirit, everyone goes to the exact same place, as there is only one. So there is no difference between Heaven and the other side.

In this book, I also want to share with you what a medium really is and what my life is like being one, as well as some of the things I have learned along the way.

But most of all, I want to help you not just to "believe" there is an afterlife, but to "know" there is one. Now you may be asking if there is a difference between the two, and there is.

To just "believe" something exists can still leave room in the mind for doubt, whereas to "know" something exists takes away all doubt.

And once you "know" that your loved ones in spirit are still with you and a part of your life, not only will this make your connection even stronger with them, but it will change your life for the better in more ways than you could ever imagine.

PART 1
BEING MEDIUM

I want to help you understand what a "medium" really is and what my personal life and experiences have been in being one.

I first want to state that I feel very fortunate being a medium and I would not change it for the world.

But being a medium is not as simple as you may think…

As you continue to read, you will see that there are experiences I have had that have enriched my life, but there have also been times that I've found having such a gift comes at a price.

The bottom line is that being a medium has changed my life in ways I never dreamed possible, as well as given me a perspective on life that I know most people do not have.

And to me that is my "gift" from God, one that I cherish in this life and will continue to cherish in the life to come.

1: What I Am, What I Do

I sometimes try to remember what my life was like before I became a medium.

It is even hard for me to recall that there was a time that I, too, actually did not know with certainty there was a God, a Heaven, or even an afterlife. Yes, I had always believed in these truths, but believing and hoping in something is a lot different than actually knowing they do in fact exist.

As you may have read in my last book, *Never Say Goodbye*, I never pictured in my wildest dreams that I was going to choose being a medium as my profession in life. Yes, as a child I had the gift, but as I became older, it took a back seat in my life while I pursued other interests. As time went on, the calling to become a medium became stronger and stronger (by the word "calling" I mean an undeniable feeling that I had to go down the path toward becoming a medium) and I gave in to it. But I also decided if I were to become a medium, I was going to do it on my own terms and in my own way… while still being me. And that is exactly what I did.

Now you may be wondering, what is the difference between a "psychic" and a "medium"?

A psychic is a person who has the ability to center in on a person's energy and receive information and impressions about them. Such things could be information about a person's past, present, and possible future events that will take place.

Believe it or not, everyone in this world possesses some level of psychic ability.

Now before you start thinking, "I'm not a psychic… Patrick, you don't know what you're talking about!" let me give you an example to illustrate how you really do possess such a skill:

I am sure you have experienced a time in your life when you knew or felt something that was about to happen and in fact it did. For instance, let's say you had a feeling that your phone was about to ring and it did. Or perhaps you were thinking about a person when all of a sudden the phone rang and it was the person you were thinking about on the other end of the line calling you. Most people do not mind claiming they have "intuition" but maintain that they are not psychic… but the two are really the same thing. Being intuitive or being psychic is simply receiving information, feelings, or impressions that are obtained neither by reason nor by perception about something or someone. And when this occurs, this is what most people generally refer to as having a "sixth sense," which is actually what it is, another sense that you have ... just like the other five that you already know about.

Your sixth sense is usually at its strongest when you are a child, but begins to decrease as you become older. The reason for this is that children's minds are not fully developed so they have to rely more on their instincts (or sixth sense) in order to understand and comprehend what is taking place around them, such as what is good, what is bad, what to do, and what not to do. But the older one becomes, the more the mind and the thinking process is used, making this instinct that was once greatly utilized as a child now less needed. So by the time one reaches adulthood, the sixth sense has become underdeveloped and that's why psychic occurrences only happen sporadically. However, in people who are known to be psychic, this sixth sense has continued to grow and become developed, and they are able to use this instinct at will.

———

What makes a medium different from a psychic is that a medium is psychic but has the additional ability of communicating one-on-one with spirits. This means that a medium can have a direct one-on-one conversation with a spirit at will.

You, yourself, actually receive messages from spirits every day, but probably are unaware most of the time when it is happening. I will discuss this further later in the book.

So to put it simply ... mediums are also psychic but psychics are not mediums.

Now as a medium, how I am able to communicate and actually receive messages from spirits is slightly more complicated to explain ... but let me give it a shot.

———

First, there are several different ways spirits will converse with me in order for me to receive and understand their messages.

The principal way I communicate with spirits is by hearing them actually speak to me. The technical term for this is called clairaudience, meaning "clear hearing." What this means is that I will hear pieces of words, whole words, and sentences, depending on the spirit. If someone was very soft spoken here in this life, they will also continue to be soft spoken in spirit. And by being so, my hearing their messages can be more challenging than, let's say, those of someone who was very loud and boisterous, who will come through loud and clear. But no matter how strong or loud a spirit's voice is, it is still extremely faint in comparison to how we hear each other here.

I remember one reading I had given; it was an early spring morning and the sun was shining brightly after a few days of rain. A woman named Jill came to me wanting to hear from her son who had passed at the age of eight. Of course my heart goes out to everyone I am giving a reading to, but especially to those who have had a child pass, as I know this is one of the hardest experiences any human being will ever have to go through in this life. We sat down and I proceeded with the reading. It took no time at all for me to start making a connection with her son, who kept running around his mom.

"Okay," I said. "Your wonderful son is making a connection with me and is telling me that you couldn't sleep last night."

Jill replied, "I couldn't sleep at all, thinking about the reading today."

I told her that I understood and asked her to try to relax.

I continued, "He's telling me that he couldn't sleep either because he was just as excited to talk with his mom. In fact, he can hardly keep still!"

We laughed even though tears started to well up in her eyes. I could see that Jill was beginning to relax and finally release the long breath that she had been holding. More at ease, she sat further back in her chair.

The reading continued with her son giving me information about his passing as well as confirmations of what he had been observing both his parents doing.

I said, "Your son is telling me something about his tummy hurting. He is saying that something was so good that he ate too much of it! Do you know what he is talking about?"

When I relayed this to her, Jill let out a gasp. She told me that on the previous night, she had made her son's favorite dessert, brownies. Anytime now when she makes them, she always sets aside a corner piece, which was always his favorite, just for him in hopes that he somehow will receive it.

"Apparently he does, and by the feeling he is giving me in my belly, maybe even a few more too!"

This confirmation put a big smile on Jill's face, not only making her happy but her son as well, as he hugged her tightly.

"I can see he is giving you a big bear hug right now," I told her and she gently patted her shoulder as if touching his arm.

I continued, "He also wants you to know that he has his wings now!"

"He was and will always be my little angel," Jill replied lovingly.

At first, I too thought he was referring to being her little angel but as she was responding, I could tell by his reaction that he was referring to something else. I asked him quietly to give me more information.

"I can tell you that your calling him your angel means the world to him and he loves you so much for that. But what he is trying to get across is something else, something about being on a plane with his dad; did your husband just take a trip?" I asked.

"Yes!" she exclaimed. "My husband was actually a pilot in the air force and still flies on weekends with some of his buddies."

"Your son wants his dad to know that he is his co-pilot now!" I confirmed.

Jill's hand trembled as she put it up to the smile on her face and said, "He always takes a picture of Chance with him and places it somewhere in the cockpit."

"And now you can let your husband know that Chance is actually riding shotgun with him in the plane!"

As the reading went on, I continued to relay to Jill what her son wanted to get across. Even though things were going well, there was something happening that kept nagging at me, something that I really didn't understand.

While speaking with Chance, even though I knew he was a young boy, the voice I kept hearing from him was like that of a teenager. It would be at a higher pitch one moment and a lower pitch the next. Even though children can and do continue to grow in spirit, I could not understand why her little boy had such a deep voice at times.

"I have to tell you something and I hope this makes sense," I told her.

Jill responded, "Please do."

"Even though I know Chance is a young boy, he's occasionally speaking to me in a deep voice."

When I mentioned this, Jill began to laugh, wiping more tears from her eyes.

She excitedly explained, "Oh, my gosh! My son used to imitate his father who has a really deep voice. We always got a kick out of that because when he did this, he knew it would make us both laugh."

I was happy to let her know that her boy was still imitating his father and to also confirm that he was still very much alive, still with them … and still trying to make them laugh.

———

A question I am also often asked is if spirits can communicate with me even if they spoke in a different language.

And the answer is yes.

Everyone in spirit is able to communicate to me in English, thank God, because that is the only language I know and I do give readings to people all over the world. Being in spirit gives people abilities they've never had before and one of them is being able to communicate in other languages. Let's just say that is one of countless "perks" of being in Heaven. But even if I am communicating with someone who spoke a language other than English, this spirit may throw in a word or two in their native tongue not only as a confirmation for their loved ones here, but also to keep me on my toes!

———

Another way a spirit can communicate with me is through what is known as clairvoyance, meaning "clear seeing." This is when a spirit will want to convey something to me visually and I will see it with my actual eyes or in my mind's eye. (And by "mind's eye," I mean it is similar to when you think about something and you envision it in your mind.) This type of communication can come in handy for spirits who want to get across a certain message that is difficult for them to put into words.

A man named Sam whose wife had passed from a car accident came to me for a reading. Not only was his wife's passing a sad occurrence for this man, but even more heartbreaking was the significance of the day the accident occurred.

As the session began, Sam shook my hand and sat down. He seemed very eager to get started and so was I as this was my first reading of the day and I was geared up, ready to go. I began like I always do by closing my eyes, taking a deep breath and waiting for the spirit to make a connection with me. Within a matter of seconds, his wife did make a connection and started to communicate with me. The first thing she did was show me an image of the car crash.

"Did your wife pass in some type of accident?" I asked.

"Yes … yes, she did," Sam said as his voice began quavering with sorrow. "Witnesses at the accident said that Jen swerved to avoid an animal in the road and ran into a tree." Body shaking, he almost couldn't get the words out.

With this, I felt so much compassion coming from his wife for her loving husband. I continued.

"Jen wants you to know that she is so very sorry for what happened. But she is also telling me that it was actually her time to pass over," I affirmed.

He grimaced and shook his head slowly.

"Jen also is telling me that her passing happened extremely quickly and she felt no pain."

He replied sadly, "That was a question I wanted to ask her."

"She said she knew that and that is why she answered it."

"That would be her," Sam replied softly.

"Jill also wants you to know that it is the truth, she says you know she would never lie to you."

Sam replied, "I've been thinking about that every minute since the accident occurred. One of the EMTs told me that she probably passed quickly but I didn't know whether to believe him or not."

"You don't have to just believe it anymore because you now know it," I assured him.

As Sam's wife continued to speak with me, she began to show me something in her hands. I couldn't make out what it was at first, but then the object she was holding finally became clear. It was a cake.

"Jen is showing me a cake; is your birthday or wedding anniversary coming up or did the accident happen around this time?" I asked.

With that, tears began streaming down his face. He turned slightly so I couldn't see the pained expression on his face.

"She died on the day of our forty-fifth wedding anniversary," he replied. "It was forty-five years of true happiness."

Sometimes there can seem to be an almost cruelty to the timing of when someone passes over. Even though the passing of a loved one is difficult enough for someone to go through, when it occurs on days that usually bring joy to a person's life, such as holidays, birthdays, and even anniversaries, it can make the passing all that much harder to endure.

I shook my head in sympathy and continued, "Jen is telling me that she knows how hard it is for you but wants you to also know that it was her time to be in spirit. She says that things like this really do happen for a reason."

"I wish I knew what those reasons were," Sam answered as he wiped his eyes.

"Jen is telling me that one day you will. She is saying that even though it is hard to understand now, timing is everything and that her passing on your anniversary is going to lead you and others down a certain path, one you would not have gone down otherwise. But she wants you to know one thing most of all—she will be going down that path with you … every step of the way."

Jen's messages continued and his spirits were lifted by the time the reading concluded. He knew that his wife was now going to be a part of his life and that she was not only going to be celebrating their wedding anniversaries together, but every day with him, always.

———

While I am giving readings, I will receive feelings or emotions from a spirit I am connecting with, which is called clairsentience, meaning "clear feelings." By spirits communicating to me in this way, they are able to convey certain messages and confirmations for the person receiving the reading. Usually this is how those in spirit will communicate their passing to me and the way they do this is by letting me feel what they felt at the time of their death, such as a giving me a pain in my heart to convey a heart attack, aches inside my body for cancer, a pounding sensation on my head for a head trauma, and so on. Keep in mind, when a spirit gives me these feelings, the impression will only last a few seconds at the most. Clairsentience is also how spirits will convey to me their personal feelings about the person who is receiving the reading as well as what their feelings are about any given subject.

One afternoon as I got ready for my next reading, I could sense a lighter atmosphere starting to develop in the room. That day Alice came to me with the hope that I would be able to make a connection with her husband Mike, whom everyone called Mikey. Alice hardly had a chance to sit down in her chair before her husband came through to me immediately. Mikey started off the conversation by laughing at something, which in turn made me laugh.

"I want you to know that it is your husband who is making me laugh," I began.

"That's him!" she said. "He would make people laugh from the moment they met him!"

"I believe it! Well, the reason I am laughing is because he is telling me to start off by saying that he is running around in Heaven with a bald head!" I stated.

This made her smile but at the same time there was a quiver in her voice as she replied, "I know he is."

Mikey let me feel pain in my head, so I knew something must have happened to him in that area. But again, keep in mind, when a spirit gives me these sensations, they only last a few seconds at most.

"Did your husband pass with some type of brain or head injury?" I asked.

She began to cry. "Yes, he did. He had to have an operation on his brain. There were complications during the procedure and he died on the operating table."

While she was saying this, Mikey kept rubbing his bald head with a big smile.

"Mikey wants you to know he did not realize that he would look so good bald!" I told her.

Again, here I was in the middle of discussing a sensitive matter and her husband kept telling jokes.

If this occurs during a reading, it sometimes can place me in an awkward position, as I never know how the person who is receiving the message is going to react. But I also understand that spirits always know what is best in what they want to communicate and the way they want to say it, so I have no choice but to just go with the flow.

After I told her what her husband had said, she burst out laughing. She managed to say, "Mikey always had the best-looking hair and would always receive compliments on it. He hated the thought of having to shave it off."

I replied, "Well, he's telling me he's going to stay bald for a while because he likes the look and … wait, he is showing me something."

At that moment, her husband started giving me a visual of his wife holding some hair in her hands.

"Do you actually still have some of his hair?" I asked.

She laughed through tears and pulled out a small plastic bag that contained pieces of his hair from her purse on the floor.

She replied, "Before his operation he had to have his head shaved and wanted me to be the one to do it. Of course, I threw the hair away, but when he died, I went back and retrieved it. I just wanted something of him to hold on to."

"He understands and loves you all the more for it," I reassured her. "But he also wants you to know that he is just thankful that you did not try to glue his hair back on his head!"

She laughed when she heard that and held the bag a bit tighter.

Again, here was her husband making us both laugh with what is usually a very sensitive subject. But that is who Mikey was and still is.

He continued making us laugh throughout the reading as well as giving Alice different confirmations, confirming his continuous connection with her. Once the reading was completed, Alice told me how much it meant to her to hear from Mikey and how much it was going to help her to know that her loving husband was always going to be with her ... even if he is now sporting a new shaved head.

———

Most mediums, when communicating with spirits, will receive messages either by clairaudience, clairvoyance, or clairsentience, but usually not all three. Let's just say it depends on what gifts the medium has personally. I feel very fortunate that I am able to communicate in all three ways as it does make it easier for me to understand the messages a spirit is conveying. Also, an interesting aspect of this process you may not realize is that it is not even up to me how a spirit will communicate ... it is up to them and their abilities. Yes, believe it or not, spirits have their own talents as well! Just as we all have our own skills in this physical world, so do they in spirit. They know what their abilities are and how best to communicate with me, so it is always up to them how they do so.

———

As a medium, I am very grateful to be able to confirm to others that life in fact does continue for their loved ones who have passed into spirit, but not everyone who comes to me wants a message from a loved one in spirit. Some people just want to have guidance and insight about their life and future, which I am also happy to help them with using my psychic abilities.

Once, a young woman named Shannon came to me in the hope that I could help her with a situation she was facing. Shannon was anticipating hearing wisdom and predictions that would help guide her, but what she received was something she was not expecting.

After I explained how I worked, I asked her which relationship she would like me to connect with.

"I really do not have anyone in spirit I would like to contact, Patrick, but is there a way you can give me some direction about an upcoming decision?" Shannon asked.

"I would be happy to do what I can for you."

"The question I have is should I pull up roots and move across the country?" she asked.

Shannon was a thirty-something-year-old woman who lived in Florida and had been offered the opportunity to be transferred to New York by her employer. She knew the move might be a good opportunity to advance her career but felt uncertain if she wanted to be so far away from her family and friends.

When someone asks me a question like this, I open myself up to their energies and see if I can pick up any information about the question asked. This can come to me with feelings that are positive or negative, as well as by seeing images in my mind's eye that might give me an indication as to what somebody should do.

In Shannon's situation, for some reason I kept seeing the image of a baby.

"Are you pregnant?" I asked.

She laughed and replied, "God, no!"

I laughed too. Again, I certainly will take someone's word for it when it comes to a question like this, but I can and will only relay what I receive … even if it doesn't make sense to the person at the time.

"Okay, for some reason I keep seeing a baby around you. Are you thinking about having one?" I asked.

"Well, I don't think so!" she said adamantly, with a grin.

"Okay, well, to get back to your original request: I don't know if this will be good news or bad news, but I am not getting that you should be moving right now. I always say, do what you want, but that is what I am picking up," I told her.

I could tell Shannon was not happy with my answer.

I always tell anyone who wants to know about their future not to ask a question to which they may not want an answer. And even though I will give someone who wants guidance what I receive, I will also tell them to always follow their own gut instincts. (We will get to "gut instincts" later on in the book.)

During Shannon's session, we talked about other subjects and I gave her my insights on those as well. At the end of her session, she thanked me for the reading but did leave seeming a bit puzzled. A few months after speaking with her, I received an e-mail from Shannon letting me know that she did in fact decide not to move away after all … and the reason?

After Shannon left me, although she wanted to move to New York, something inside was telling her not to. A few weeks had passed and, still being in an undecided state of mind, she unexpectedly met up with an old flame from school. The two started dating and rekindled their romance, falling deeply in love. A whirlwind marriage took place soon after.

Shannon was also expecting her first child.

In the e-mail she thanked me for her reading. She was amazed by how quickly her life had changed.

Shannon's life had completely transformed within a matter of only months and in a way she never dreamt of. Though her mind was telling her to move across country, there was something inside her telling her (not just me) not to do so. And by listening to her gut instinct, she was in the happiest place of her life.

———

Even though being psychic gives me the ability to pick up on certain aspects of the path someone is going down, it is still always up to the individual to decide where that path is going to eventually take them.

2: Medium Misconceptions

I was once asked by someone if it drives me crazy to constantly hear the voices of spirits in my head.

I must admit that I had to laugh when they asked me this, and I said that I am not some sort of schizophrenic and that I actually do not hear voices in my head all the time.

I could picture this individual thinking that when I am walking around, I am constantly hearing spirits in my head telling me to give this person or that person a message. Believe me, if that were the case, I would probably go insane … and spirits realize this too! Keep in mind spirits are still people and most of them will respect my abilities by only connecting and speaking with me when I want them to. (Notice I used the word "most," as there can be a spirit every now and then who does not follow my rules!)

Of course I know people could think this way because of a preconceived notion of what they believe a medium to be from what they have seen on television shows and in films. Some of the more popular television shows in recent history like *Medium* and *Ghost Whisperer* have had mediums as their featured characters who are constantly bombarded by spirits.

This really does not happen in real life.

Fictional mediums on television and in movies are made-up characters who have been Hollywoodized. (I'm coining that word here … meaning someone or something Hollywood has created or exaggerated for entertainment purposes.) This tends to be true even if the character of the medium has been factually based on a real-life person. A good example of this is when other television shows or movies feature characters such as doctors or lawyers. Actual doctors and lawyers will tell you that these shows and movies never come close to what it is actually like being in that particular profession … the same goes with mine.

But this question did have me wondering what some of the other perceptions and misconceptions are about me being a medium. So let me take on a few.

MISCONCEPTION: THAT I SEE DEAD PEOPLE EVERYWHERE I GO

Just as above, with some believing that I hear spirits all the time, some people also think that I see spirits everywhere I go, and this is not the case. They envision that, when I am out in public, I see spirits walking around in stores, at the airport, or even at the beach.

Are there spirits at these locations?

Of course there are, as spirits are with their loved ones at various times no matter where a person may be. But just like above with hearing spirits, even though I may at times spot a spirit here and there in public, I do not see them everywhere all the time.

There have been many times when I have been stopped on the street by people who ask me if there are spirits around them. To have some fun with that question, I will usually say that the only spirit I see around them is a large, looming one who is draped in a black robe and holding a sickle telling me to let them know that they will see them soon! It is comical how wide a person's eyes will get when I say this and people will then ask me quickly if I am kidding. When I say that I am, with a big sigh of relief they will tell me they thought I was serious.

One time while grocery shopping, Kathy and I noticed a woman who seemed to have been following us through the store. Though it is not uncommon for me to be recognized from time to time in public, usually a person will come up and say hi and ask for an autograph, which is happily given.

With this person, every time we would walk down a different aisle in the store, eventually she too would end up in that same aisle, staring at us. We figured she knew who we were and was just shy, so we would smile if our eyes made contact and continued shopping. After going down a few more aisles, the woman seemed to have worked up enough nerve to finally make her way to us. With a bashful smile on her face, she said in a very quiet voice that she knew who we were and that she loved our work. We told her she was very kind to tell us that and thanked her for the compliment, but before we could get another word in she abruptly asked me if I saw any spirits with her.

My mind at that time was on shopping and making sure I was not going to forget the milk, so I was not concentrating on the spirits walking around. I kindly told her I was not opened at that moment and that I did not see any spirits around her. With my reply, a shocked look came across her face and she then asked if I was sure. I affirmed that I was very sure but if a spirit did come to me while I was buying bread, I would certainly let her know. She laughed and thanked me, but I could tell that she was a bit surprised that I was not seeing any of her dead relatives with her in the supermarket. Again, it is not that her loved ones were not with her; I was just not open to them at that time.

In order for me to make a full connection with spirits and actually communicate with them, I have to be in my "on" state. Again, it is difficult to explain exactly what that means, but basically my senses are opened up and I place myself in a zone. By zone, I am not talking about being in a trance, but let's just say I have to be in a state of deep concentration.

Could I walk around in this state and then see dead people all around me everywhere I go?

Yes, but I wouldn't do this. The reason is that it takes a great deal of energy in order to be in this state and the longer that I am in it, the more draining it becomes on my body.

So before I give a reading, I do take a few moments to get into the zone and once I am finished, I leave that state.

And besides, I really do not want to communicate with spirits while I am grocery shopping; they may want to give me their shopping list and Kathy's is long enough!

MISCONCEPTION: SPIRITS MAKE ALL OF MY LIFE DECISIONS

Sometimes people think that because I am able to communicate with spirits that they make all of my decisions in life for me.

Ha, if only that were true.

Just because I am able to communicate with those who are in Heaven does not mean that I have a dependency on them for making my life decisions. Besides, they wouldn't do so anyway.

The reason we are all here in the first place is that we need to understand and experience certain truths and events in our lives, good and bad, in order for our souls to grow, and this is done with every decision we make on this Earth. That includes even me. And if you think about it, you are the person you are today because of every decision you have made. Each choice, each thought you have ever had or ever made has resulted in making you, you.

I recall one time I was speaking with my mom and dad who are in spirit and asked them for advice. A certain heavy metal radio station in Texas wanted me to come on their morning show and give readings to their listeners on air. I always enjoy giving interviews and readings on the radio, but a heavy metal music format was not the typical radio station type that would ask me to be on as the demographics of their listening audience were more into head banging than mediums. So for fun, I asked my parents for advice on whether or not I should do this interview. They would not give me a yes or no and said it was up to me.

So I decided to go ahead with the interview as I enjoy taking on a challenge and I had a feeling that I was about to have one. These kind of "zoo" morning shows usually have good interviews with me, but since this was a heavy metal-themed one and had a reputation of making fun of their guests, I knew I'd better be prepared for anything.

The hosts came on the phone and welcomed me to their show. They explained who I was to their audience and asked me a few questions about what it is that I do. With these shows, there is usually one person who is skeptical, which is fine as I not only understand this, but expect it. But with these hosts, I could tell by their questioning and snickering that all of them were pretty much non-believers, which again was fine by me, just so long as they gave me a chance to prove them wrong.

After the questioning, it was time to take callers. The hosts placed the first one on the phone and I started to give out the messages that I was receiving for this person. I could tell that the caller was extremely nervous and it was hard for him to even respond to any of my comments. Anytime I told him something, his responses to me were either not an answer or he would say he was not sure. This went on for a few minutes and I told the caller just to think about what

I had told him and I thanked him for calling. As soon as I finished with him, the hosts, who were laughing, stated that during the reading, every time the caller hesitated or said he was not sure, they would play a loud buzzer sound, as if I had gotten the information wrong. The thing that they thought was the funniest was that I was unable to hear the buzzer on my end of the phone so I was unaware of what was actually taking place. Even though I did not find it amusing, I knew this type of show had to be "entertaining" and perform such novelty pranks on their guests. So I told the hosts that I could tell that the caller was not only very nervous about being on the radio, but also hearing from his father in spirit. They thought about what I said for a second and admitted that was possible.

I then decided to turn it around to them.

I told the hosts that since they were not nervous about being on the radio, I would try to speak with one of their relatives in spirit. I could tell by their silence that this took them by surprise, and finally one of the hosts said that he would volunteer and asked if I could speak with his grandfather.

I took a moment and asked within for his grandfather to make a connection with me. I was hoping that his grandfather would come as I wanted to not only show these hosts that I can do what I say I can do, but to also give them a taste of their own medicine. And then his grandfather did in fact make a connection with me.

I was pleased that his grandfather was a good communicator and able to get through not only his name, but he told me things about himself and his grandson that only they would have known. It was as if this grandfather was trying to prove a point. You could hear a pin drop in the silence from the hosts as they all could not believe what was actually taking place.

So after I completed the reading, I asked them where the buzzer was now. Still acting as their radio personas, they told me that I really freaked them out and that there was in fact something to what it is that I do.

Later I received an e-mail from the person I gave a reading to on the air. He told me that he was sorry that he was unable to speak on the radio as he was in shock from hearing the messages he had received. He told me that after he'd hung up, he called his mother and that the information he had received during his short reading helped not only his mother, but his entire family immensely.

The bottom line is that if my parents had told me that games were going to be played during my interview with this radio show, I may not have decided to go on. But when I did, not only was I able to help the caller and his family, but I was also able to put some radio show hosts in their place. (I have to admit, I love when that happens.)

So now, you may be wondering, are my loved ones in spirit able to give me any advice at all? Of course they are.

Everyone on this Earth receives guidance from their loved ones in spirit, one way or another, I just have a more direct way of receiving it. Spirits help people by placing thoughts in their heads (I wonder where that idea came from?) as well as a gut instinct to do something. But living this life requires all of us to make many of our own personal decisions on how and what we do ... even me.

By the way, the radio station did contact me a few days later and said they would love to have me back on the air as soon as possible ... I politely declined.

MISCONCEPTION:
I MEDITATE CONSTANTLY

To be honest, I have never been one to sit on the ground with my legs crossed, arms on my lap, palms out, eyes closed, and say "Ommmmmmmm" out loud. Not that there is anything wrong with those who do, it is just not for me.

When I first started to develop my skills as a medium, I knew I had to learn about and practice meditation. I came to the understanding that meditating would help me learn how to quiet my mind and by doing so actually help make my communication with spirits even stronger. I have to tell you that this was not an easy task for me. I had never meditated before, but I was going to give it a try.

At first, I listened to various styles of CDs and read many books on the subject of meditation. Most of the concepts that I read about bored me so much that I felt like I was going into a meditative state just reading them. (Hmmm, maybe that was the point.) I remember one CD instructed me to picture myself as a piece of wood. (Yes, you read that correctly, I said a piece of wood.) And while in the state of being a piece of wood (by the way, the narrator never said what kind of wood I was supposed to be, walnut, oak, or cherry, but I digress ...), I was then supposed to lie back and think of myself as floating in water. But the way my mind works, I kept thinking, why can I not just picture myself lying in water, why do I also have to be a piece of wood? So by analyzing everything, I could never get into it and relax. But I knew that I had to learn how to meditate somehow, so what I decided to do was to make the meditation more "normal." If the meditation called for me to picture myself in a pyramid, I would just picture myself sitting on the beach. If the meditation called for me to think of myself in great chambers in some high kingdom, I would just think of myself... on the beach. (Hey, what can I say, I like the beach...)

The point is that whatever meditation I came across, I would somehow turn it into an exercise I was comfortable with, and by doing so, I was in fact able to learn how to concentrate more and to quiet my mind. I also found that the more I meditated, the faster I was able to reach that point of consciousness for communication with spirit, and the meditation sessions actually became shorter and shorter as time went on.

Today, anytime I am about to give a reading, I take a few minutes to relax and clear my mind, which helps me to open myself up for the session... but this really is the only "formal" meditation that I now do.

Unless watching reality shows counts, too...

MISCONCEPTION: SPIRITS "JUMP" INTO MY BODY

If you recall, in the movie *Ghost*, Whoopi Goldberg played a medium who would go into a trance-like state and have spirits jump into her body in order for them to communicate with their loved ones.

The common term used when a medium makes a connection with a spirit is "channeling," which means communicating with spirits. But due to what is seen on television shows and in movies, people have the misconception that when I channel a spirit, that spirit has to jump into my body in order for them to communicate. This does not happen to me as spirits do not jump into and take over my body when I am communicating with them.

I have to admit that I too was unsure about how this channeling stuff worked when I first started looking into becoming a medium. Even though I personally always had my doubts that this is what actually took place, I still needed to know for sure. As you can imagine, the thought of having a spirit take over my body made me weary about becoming a medium. (Hey, I saw those television shows and movies, too.) So as I developed into becoming a medium, I found out for certain that any communication I had with spirits did not involve possession.

When I "channel," a spirit will come and make a connection with me and then the communication will begin. The way this happens is that spirits will either stand next to me or beside their loved ones who are receiving the reading, and I will then communicate with them. What I will do is open my "sixth sense" up by raising my vibration to a very high level. The spirits will work with me in order to make a connection by lowering their vibrations, thereby making it possible for our energies to connect and the communication to take place. It takes a great deal of energy on my part to do this and sustain it for a long period of time, which is why I need to pace myself when giving readings.

So do spirits actually enter the body of anyone or any medium? In my opinion, no. I believe there can be a very strong "connection" between a spirit and a person, but not an actual takeover of the body. (But that sure would explain sometimes why some people act the way they do.)

MISCONCEPTION: I GO INTO A TRANCE WHEN GIVING READINGS

As far as being in a trance state, that can go either way depending on your definition of a trance. If you think of a trance as when mediums are totally unaware of and unresponsive to what is taking place around them and not in control over what is happening to them, then no, I am not in a trance. I would say, however, that when giving a reading, I am in a deep state of concentration.

When communicating with those on the other side, I have to focus solely on the conversation taking place with a spirit. This requires concentration and I do have to shut off my awareness of what is happening around me. At no time, though, do I ever lose control of myself, my body, or am I unable to snap out of my concentration.

One time I had ten people attend a short reading. These groups usually last around two hours with each participant receiving a ten- to fifteen-minute reading. Most people who attend such groups are usually not only excited to receive their own reading, but also take pleasure in listening to the other readings I'm giving as well. In this one group, I was about an hour and a half into it and had only a few more people left to read. As I started making a connection with them and was deep in concentration, I started hearing the sound of someone crunching on a snack. At first I tried to not to pay attention to it, but you know how it goes, the more you try not to hear something, the louder it becomes. So I turned in the direction the sound was coming from and saw a woman who had already received her reading, munching on some potato chips! I looked at her and she looked at me with a surprised look on her face and told me that she was sorry; she thought I was in a trance and I would not hear her chomping away. I replied that not only did I hear her, but the spirits did too, and if she did not put those chips down, the spirits were going to haunt her. (I like to scare people a little who misbehave.) She got a terrified look and I told her that I was kidding, but she did need to stop what she was doing, which she was happy to do.

So at any of my events I have a sign that reads "No Chips Allowed!" ... just kidding. (But really, don't bring chips!)

MISCONCEPTION: I "PULL" THE SPIRIT FROM HEAVEN TO ME TO COMMUNICATE

Some people believe that when I am giving a reading, I will somehow "command" a spirit to come and speak with me and by doing so, they must leave wherever they are and come directly to me. It is like they think I have special powers and am able to pull a spirit out of Heaven to come and communicate with their loved ones here.

Are you kidding me?

The truth is that even though spirits are in Heaven they also continue to participate in this life as well. When giving a reading, I will open myself up and then ask what relationship the person receiving a reading would like me to connect with. I never have a problem in connecting with a spirit a person wants to speak with as the spirit already knows what is taking place and is prepared to interact with me. (More than likely they are the ones who arranged the reading anyway.)

Again, it is one of those things that people see from the stories dreamed up in Hollywood, which are only for dramatic purposes. Sometimes when Kathy and I are giving demonstrations, just for fun she or I will call out in a very dramatic voice that we "summon the spirit world to tear open the veil and bring forth messages from beyond the grave!" Of course this is done just to make the audience laugh and to show how ridiculous that concept really is.

So no, I do not have to force, nor could I, any spirit to come and speak with me because someone here wants to communicate with them. Remember that loved ones in spirit are just as excited to speak with their loved ones as the people here are!

MISCONCEPTION: I KNOW EVERYTHING THAT IS GOING TO HAPPEN

People assume that mediums and psychics know all, and this is simply false.

Being a medium and psychic, even though I am able to pick up on certain events that may have taken place or will take place in a person's life, or even something that may take place in the world, this does not mean I know every-thing. And if a medium or psychic tells you they do … they are lying to you, as there is no one in this world who is able to do so.

Many people feel when significant tragedies take place, such as massive earthquakes or floods, psychics should know they are going to happen before they do. Yes, there can in fact be times when a psychic can sense something tragic is about to take place, and even predict the time and location … but these occasions are very few and far between. Why? Because it is through these negative events occurring in the world that our souls have the opportunity to learn and grow.

Recently Kathy and I were at an airport waiting for a plane to take us to New York City. It was very early in the morning and the airport seemed particularly busy for that time of day so we figured everyone just wanted to get an early start, like us.

After long lines at security and Kathy shopping at the magazine shop for what seemed like an eternity, we finally made it to our gate. While we were sitting there a young man came over and introduced himself to us. He was excited to see us as he said he recently had attended one of our in-person events. We asked if he enjoyed it and he told us he had. He said he was a guest of someone who dragged him there and he was a bit skeptical in the begin-ning, but what he witnessed that night really gave him much to think about. We told him that there's nothing wrong with being skeptical, just as long as he's open for his mind to be changed, to which he agreed.

As we were finishing our conversation, we heard the dreaded announcement come over the gate terminal loud-speaker that our flight was going to be delayed. Of course we all said, "Oh great," but we hoped that it was not going to take too long. After the announcement was made, the young man we were speaking with turned to me and said that I should have known that the plane was going to be late because I was a psychic. Smiling, I responded that even though I might know when specific events will take place, that does not mean I know everything that is going to happen in this world. He shrugged his shoulders, nodded his head, and said what I told him made sense.

As he started to walk away I told him to be careful to watch what he ate on the plane. He looked at me puzzled, and asked me why, was there going to be something wrong with his food? Kathy laughed as I waited a moment for him to consider what I had said to him. Then I let him off the hook and told him no … it's airplane food and you don't have to be psychic to know how bad it is going to be!

So even though I may have a heads up on much of what is going to happen to people and even events that may be taking place, I do not know everything … nor would I ever want to.

MISCONCEPTION: I BELIEVE WHAT OTHER MEDIUMS BELIEVE

Some people think that mediums for the most part all act on and believe in the same things.

This is absolutely not true.

But I can understand where that misconception may have come from. If mediums are speaking with spirits who are on the other side, wouldn't spirits express what Heaven is like all in the same way?

Not exactly.

It's like this; we all live our lives on this Earth and share the same air, space, and time. But what makes this world a unique experience for each of us is our own personal "perspective," giving us all a different point of view. This also works the same way with mediums.

Every medium communicates with spirits in their own individual way and by doing so, it is up to the medium how they interpret what the spirits are communicating and how they will perceive the meaning of the messages.

At times I have seen other mediums on television, and he or she could be saying something or even doing something that I do not agree with. I remember once seeing a "so-called" medium (I use the term "so-called" because I do not believe that this person is really a medium) on a television show. This medium, along with a team of people, went to a house where a young girl was supposedly possessed by a demon. This medium and the group of people started to yell at this girl and demand that the demon leave her body. She began screaming while rolling around on the floor alongside her parents, who were watching this take place. With much persistence from the group, the demon supposedly left the girl. I know, I know, it sounds like the movie *The Exorcist*, but this was a paranormal television show and the event was supposed to be real.

I just shook my head in disbelief.

I do not believe in demons, nor do I believe in what is known as a person being possessed, but apparently this medium did. What I do believe in is that there are people who have real mental issues and there are people out there calling themselves mediums taking advantage of them. But even though I did not believe the above medium was real, there are other mediums whom I do believe to be real and whom I also disagree with.

What I believe, know, and understand about this life and the afterlife is an accumulation of all of the personal experiences I have had in this physical life as well as what I have learned from speaking with spirit.

That, along with a large dose of common sense mixed in…

Misconception: New-age type people are the only ones into mediums

Another misconception many have comes in not knowing how people in every walk of life are really interested in mediumship and the work both Kathy and I do.

When I first became a medium, both Kathy and I were living in California, and for anyone who has never been there, it is different than any other part of the country, in a good way. People who live in California, especially southern California, for the most part do their own thing and are less concerned by the views of others. So being a medium or having an alternative view of religion in Los Angeles is not considered out of the ordinary at all.

Once while on a trip back home to Virginia, Kathy and I were asked to appear on a local television show to talk about what we do. Being from the South, we knew that religious views are very strong and straightforward there. There are churches on practically every street corner and many attend one. And even though there are a variety of religions in the South, the majority of people are Christians and both Kathy and I were curious on how our work might go over there. We knew the show we were asked to appear on also had a conservative audience and we were curious about the response we would receive. But we have always been ones to throw caution to the wind and wanted to let everyone see that speaking with spirits really isn't all that strange, so we decided to go for it!

So both Kathy and I were interviewed on the show and answered questions about the work we do as well as questions about the afterlife. The producers had also lined up several people who received a reading from me.

After the taping was over, the host thanked us both and said that she appreciated our taking the time to appear on her show. We told her it was our pleasure and that we were happy that this show was going to shed some light on what we represent. She agreed. I asked the host when she thought the show was going to air and she said that it would be sometime in October. I laughed and told her of course it would … just in time for Halloween.

Fortunately, due to good timing, Kathy and I happened to be back in Virginia at the time our story was going to air and once it did, to our amazement, not only did we not receive one negative response from viewers, but it was quite the opposite...

We were floored by the many positive calls, letters, and e-mails we received from people from every walk of life! From farmers, lawyers, to even people who ran those churches on the corner (those who would be deemed "conservative") all of these people were extremely happy with and very supportive of what Kathy and I do! Many of them thanked us for helping them to understand that they were not crazy when thinking that they were still connected with their loved ones in spirit!

Not long after the show aired, we received an e-mail from the host of the show letting us know that our story received the most calls and letters of any story they had ever produced.

So yes, one of the goals that Kathy and I have always wanted to achieve and feel we have helped achieve is to bring mediumship "out of the closet" and into the twenty-first century and to show that mediums and the subject of the afterlife is not just for "new-agers" anymore!

3: The Skeptical Medium

I have one of the only jobs in the world where I must constantly and consistently prove that I am able to do what I say I can do ... and believe it or not, I certainly understand why!

Mediums claim they are able to do something very few people are actually capable of doing and what some people even think is impossible: being able to communicate with spirits. So I never take offense when people are skeptical, just so long they are open skeptics and willing to give me a chance to change their minds.

But people are sometimes quite surprised to hear that I too can be very skeptical when it comes to other mediums. And why shouldn't I be?

I have dedicated and sacrificed much in my life to being a medium and take offense when others try to pass themselves off as something they are not. Let's just face the facts; there are frauds out there claiming to be mediums when they are not. Not only do these people give mediums a bad name, some of them are also taking advantage of those in need.

Being a medium, you can say I am an "expert" on the subject matter as well as the profession, knowing what it actually takes to be one. And with this, I can easily spot a fake from a mile away.

———

I was recently watching a paranormal show that featured several so-called mediums sitting around a table trying to make connections with famous people. From Marilyn Monroe to Clark Gable, these mediums were going to bring through the Hollywood elite and share their messages from beyond the grave. The room was dark, of course, and they were calling out, trying to command these famous people to come forth to bring a message. Let me tell you, if I were ever to try to "command" a spirit to come and speak with me, the only thing I would hear coming from their end would be laughter!

Okay, when seeing what was taking place, I knew that the "dramatics" were only the beginning and could not wait to see what was coming next. To add to the eeriness, the room where this séance was taking place was rumored to be haunted by a person who hung himself there.

As this session continued, at first nothing was happening. The so-called mediums kept calling out but no spirit was making a connection or making their presence known. But after a few more minutes, and knowing time was ticking by... suddenly it happened! One of the so-called mediums, a female, started to channel the person who had hung himself right in that very room! This woman had a glazed look in her eyes as if she was in some type of deep trance, of course along with heavy breathing. As this woman sat in her trance-like state, she grabbed her throat as if she was being strangled and she uttered a few words, saying to the effect that she was being hung!

Of course, just as with any "actor," the other so-called mediums who were also sitting around the table were not going to let her steal the spotlight.

The next female medium around the table also started going into a trance, channeling the same person. She started to give messages from this person and stated that the location of the hanging took place in a corner of the room where they were sitting and she pointed to the spot.

The first medium, not to be outdone, stated that it did not take place in that corner and insisted they were actually sitting under the location of the hanging! The second medium, forgetting that she was supposed to be in a trance, started to argue with the first medium, maintaining that she did in fact see someone hanging in the corner of the room.

I could not stop laughing at how ridiculous this whole scenario was, knowing what it is actually like to connect with a spirit and how a real medium would not be reacting this way if it were in fact taking place. But the show was not over yet.

To top it off, a third medium at the table started to have a go at it, thrusting his body back and forth in a chair, and he too was unable to catch his breath. He started calling out messages from the hung spirit, stating how much pain this poor soul was still in.

The messages continued to go back and forth with each medium and soon they got so tangled up in their stories that they lost track of who was saying what and decided that there must be more than one spirit with whom they were speaking.

Again, I could not stop laughing at how funny as well as ridiculous this was. How easy would it be for a medium at a session to make grunting noises and nonsensical statements that add up to nothing? But it takes a lot more than that to prove to people that communicating with spirits is for real.

While I was watching this whole fiasco taking place, the scariest part was knowing that a large number of the people out there actually believed what they were watching was real. And thus, they come to the conclusion that all mediums act in this manner.

———

Being a "real" medium takes much more than theatrics; in fact, it is not theatrical at all. A legitimate medium needs to do one thing and one thing only, and that is to bring messages from those in spirit containing meaningful confirmations that the receiver or viewing audience can verify. So, one of my goals as a medium is to break any stereotypes that people may associate with the gift and to show that real mediums do not need any of that hocus pocus stuff to communicate with the other side.

Even though you can describe those above mediums as just actors who are entertaining viewers on a television show and nothing else, there are others out there who are not just entertaining, but actually taking advantage of people in need.

———

I once spoke with a woman who connected with her family in spirit. After a while, I could sense she had something on her mind that she had been suffering with for a long time. When I asked her what it was, she told me that she had been to a medium before and was told that she had a curse placed on her by a jilted boyfriend. She said that ever since she was told this, she'd had nothing but bad luck. Some of the incidents that had happened to her recently were that she had a flat tire as well as slipping at home and hurting her ankle. She said the medium told her that in order to stop having bad luck she would have to pay the medium an exorbitant sum to remove the curse.

It is frauds like this that really make my blood boil.

I knew how ridiculous all of this was and told this woman that there are no such things as curses. I also explained that if all of these negative occurrences were due to a curse, then everyone in this world is cursed as we all have bad things happen to us. I clarified that it's the same for us all; if you focus on any one thing, you are going to notice it more acutely. An example of this is to go outside and tell yourself you are going to observe everything that is red … you will see more red objects, such as red cars, red shoes, red shirts, etc. So by only concentrating on negative things that were happening in her life, I told her, she would amplify them, making it seem as if there were a lot more. I stated that, in my opinion, she would just be throwing her money away if she gave it to this woman to remove a curse.

The woman thanked me and I could tell that she was relieved. But I also knew there are many more people out there that have and will fall for the same cons that these criminals pull on the vulnerable.

———

So yes, I understand why there are skeptics out there and I am proud to include myself as one of them. It makes those of us who are real showcase what our gifts are and helps people to know the differences between what is real and what is false.

And by the way, those so-called mediums above on that television show never did make a connection with any celebrities…

4: MEDIUM CHALLENGES

Not so long ago, I was at a family reunion and having a discussion with one of my sister-in-laws about my work. She mentioned that one of her neighbors was having trouble with her marriage and the neighbor was wondering if there was any guidance I could give her through a reading. I replied that her neighbor should contact me. With that, my sister-in-law asked me, "You deal with that, too? I didn't think that was the kind of work you did."

Most people do not realize that as a medium, you wear many hats when giving a reading. Though many times it is acting a conduit between a person and a loved one in spirit, confirming their everlasting life, love, and presence ... there are many times when it can be much more than that. Issues I deal with range from marriages in trouble, people lost in their life, to those who are even on the edge of committing suicide. The list can go on and on. As a medium I not only listen and try to help those who are going through these difficulties, but I also take on the energy that surrounds them and I have to tell you—at times this can be very challenging.

———

I recall one time picking up the phone for an appointment and when I said hello, the only thing I heard on the other end was a woman named Lindsey crying. When I asked her to calm down and told her that everything was going to be all right, Lindsey started to scream at me, "He's dead! He's dead! It is not going to be all right!" When I asked who was dead, she replied that her boyfriend Steve had been killed in an automobile accident as she continued to sob.

So I asked Lindsey in a calm voice to take a few deep breaths and as she did, I could feel that her boyfriend in spirit was starting to make a connection with me. As Lindsey regained her composure, I asked if she would like me to speak with Steve. I could tell by his presence that he had a lot to say to her and when she agreed, I began the reading.

"Your boyfriend wants you to know first that he is safe and sound," I said.

"Steve was always a good driver; I don't understand why he had to die!" Lindsey said with anger in her voice.

With that Steve started to let me sense the feeling of drugs running through my body.

"I feel that Steve must have been intoxicated or using drugs when he passed over," I replied.

"Yes, he had been on a drinking binge with some of his buddies and got into an argument at a bar. He stormed out angry, got into a car, and ran into a building." She started to cry again.

"Okay, calm down," I said. "Steve wants you to know how sorry he is, that it was a stupid thing for him to do. You know how headstrong he is, but he wants you to know that he still loves you very much."

After a moment more of weeping, she cried out, "Well, I want to be with him!"

Steve and I felt the same concern as we heard those words and we both knew that she was on the verge of taking her own life. I could also feel the love and compassion Steve had for her and knew that he was ready to convey his message for her.

"Steve is saying how much you meant to him and still do. But he also wants you to know that you cannot be with him in spirit at this time," I relayed

"Why not?" she screamed. "I know if I kill myself I will be with him again!"

"Yes, even though you would also be in spirit, it would not be the way you imagine; in fact, it would be the opposite. By taking your life, you are changing the course of your journey and with that, all that you are still meant to do and accomplish. Once in spirit, you will be aware of this and very much regret what has taken place, along with seeing and feeling the consequences of your actions with those who love you and whom you have left behind. Also, keep in mind, not only will you be robbing yourself of these lessons, but Steve as well. In spirit, Steve is not only going to continue to love you, but will also be helping you in ways you could never conceive. This will not only benefit you, but also Steve's spirit. Steve is also telling me how lovingly stubborn you can be and insists that you be stubborn about living!"

I could tell that finally this was getting through to Lindsey.

"I just don't think I can continue to go on. My heart is breaking and my soul aches to be with him."

"Steve wants you to know that your heart is breaking because of the love you have for him, and that love is actually a part of him in spirit. As you continue with your life, your heart will not only heal, but you will find that you are not living life alone and that Steve is a part of it. These are truths you will become aware of as you allow the healing process to begin."

By now I could sense Lindsey started to take Steve's message to heart. Her voice had become calmer.

"I just do not know where to start," she replied.

With this, Steve showed me a visual in my mind's eye of Lindsey lying in bed.

"Have you not been out since Steve's accident?" I asked. "Steve is showing me that you are in bed."

"No, I have not gone out. I just wanted to be alone," Lindsey told me.

I know that when I am taking private appointments, the average waiting time is months in advance for someone to receive one, and I was surprised that Lindsey had been bedridden for so long. When I mentioned this to her, both she and Steve started talking to me at the same time. I asked Steve to hold on so I could understand Lindsey.

Lindsey said that when she made her appointment, she was told that it usually takes months to receive one, but it so happened that someone had to change their appointment that very day and she only had to wait a few weeks. I was happy to hear that she had not been in bed for any longer than that length of time and next I began to concentrate on what else Steve had to say.

"Steve is telling me that he is the one who arranged your earlier appointment and that this is just one of many ways he is helping you. He is telling me that you have to believe him when he says that your circumstances are going to get better and he wants you out of that bed!"

I had noticed that during the reading her sobbing became less and less intense. When Lindsey heard what Steve had to tell her, she responded in a hopeful voice, "Okay, I will get out if he wants me to."

"He does, he says. There's so much out there for you, for both of you to do, and he is ready to take on the next adventure with you."

"He would always say that!" Lindsey shouted. "He hated to be stuck in the house and always wanted to go out on an adventure!"

"Well, he still does!" I told her. "And he will still be doing it right along with you!"

After hearing that as well as several other messages from Steve, Lindsey told me that she'd actually started to feel his presence with her during our conversation and knew that he was with her. She promised both me and Steve that she would not take her life and believed that her life would get better. A year or so later I did speak with

Lindsey again and her life was indeed much brighter. She told me that she had decided to go back to school and even though she missed Steve very much with her in this physical realm, she knew he was with her and could even feel how proud he was of her.

That made two of us.

———

So there are many times when my job as a medium involves more than confirming the existence of a loved one in spirit. I must be ready, open, and willing to take on a host of situations that a person may be going through and hopefully be able to help them get back on track. At times, this can become very emotional, not only for the person receiving the reading, but for myself as well.

I take every reading I give to heart, and take comfort in knowing that what I do … I am not doing alone.

5: BECOMING EMOTIONALLY INVOLVED

Through my work I have come across a variety of people, each having reasons for why they want to receive a reading from me. There are some who come to see me who are at a happy place in their lives and just want to say hi to a parent or grandparent in spirit and hear messages from them. These readings can stir up many positive emotions, from happiness and laughter to excitement.

But then there are those whom I give readings to who are suffering greatly due to an unexpected passing of someone they love. These readings are usually with those who are agonizing in great pain and my heart truly goes out to them … as well as my empathy.

As a medium, it is my job to maintain my composure, and I try to keep myself in check while giving a reading as I want to be able to fully concentrate on what I am doing. But the trouble is that I am not only a medium, but also

Patrick. And sometimes during a reading my emotions can overtake the medium in me, reacting to what is transpiring around me.

An example of this is when I spoke with Martin and Patricia, a couple who wanted me to make a connection with their twin boys Trey and Taylor. Their sons were fun-loving ten-year-old boys who were known for their charisma and charm and got along with everyone, even at that age.

When I begin a session and make a connection with spirits, I try to set up guidelines on how I want to start the reading and, for the most part, the spirits will usually follow my lead. The very first thing I will ask a spirit to do is to communicate their passing to me and this is usually done by letting me feel what they went through. These two young boys were going to do this reading their way, however.

"Your sons are starting to make a connection with me and I can tell you that I already feel that I am going to have trouble with them," I told their parents with a grin.

"We had a feeling you just might," said Martin as he held Patricia's hand.

I continued with, "Your boys are breaking my rules and they keep speaking together at the same time, so right now I will just have to combine their messages together."

The couple offered a chuckle and nodded.

"First, they both want you to know not only how very excited they are that you are doing this, but most of all how much they love you and that they are still your boys, even in spirit."

This is not an unusual message for me to hear, but it is something that will usually come more often toward the end of a reading. Since Trey and Taylor were taking the lead, they wanted this to be the very first words out of their mouths and with that, both parents started to tear up.

"These boys were our lives, our everything," said Patricia.

"Well, they want you to know that they still are," I stated. "This is important for you to understand, they are telling me."

I knew what the boys wanted to do, to tell their parents that they were not only still alive, but still their beautiful sons. But I also know that when someone comes to me for a reading, it is important to start it out by giving some form of validation that I am actually making a connection and speaking with their loved ones in spirit. By doing so, any messages that are given become all the more powerful. So to myself, I quietly asked Trey and Taylor again how they passed over as a confirmation for their parents, and this time they answered.

"Your boys are now giving me a sense of their passing," I told the couple.

The mood in the room intensified.

I began to experience a cold feeling deep inside along with the sensation of being pulled down. I told the couple what I was experiencing and with that, the tears really started to flow.

"I'm so sorry. Do you want me to go on?" I asked, seeing how upset Martin and Patricia were becoming.

"Yes, please do, please continue," replied Martin.

"Okay. Your boys keep giving me this feeling of falling and being freezing cold, did they freeze to death?" I asked.

Patricia responded, still weeping, "My poor babies, they went outside to play in the snow, something they had done so many times before. They strayed farther than they ever had and somehow ended up walking on top of a pond. It was also covered in snow. The ice gave out underneath them and they both drowned."

Once she said that, they started to sob uncontrollably as Martin looked up and started shouting, "Why, God, why did you take our boys from us?" He put his head down and Patricia rubbed his shoulder.

Now I understood why the boys wanted to start off the reading the way they did. Trey and Taylor wanted their parents to realize that God did not in fact take them away and that they were still very much with them. But I also understood at the same time the pain that Martin and Patricia were in, as having a child, much less two of them, pass is the hardest thing any human being will ever have to go through in this life. With what was taking place, my eyes too began to fill with tears. Here was a loving family who seemed to be doing everything right. Two hardworking parents dedicating their lives to making sure that their kids were well fed, educated, and loved. In a matter of only an hour, their lives were completely turned upside down, never to be the same again. I could just imagine the terrible thoughts playing out over and over again in their heads of those two beautiful young boys going out just to have some fun in the snow when sudden tragedy struck with the ice collapsing underneath their feet, both drowning. I also knew that there was not a day that did not go by that Martin and Patricia did not ask the same question

I'd just heard from Martin—"Why?" And even though I know there are reasons for such tragedies to happen in people's lives, I still have compassion and my heart aches for those who go through them.

After I offered the couple a box of tissues, I took a tissue myself and wiped the tears from my face. I then reached out to these two in such pain and held both of their hands. I regained my composure and continued with my connection with their sons.

"I want you to know that your boys are now pointing at each other and are telling me that even though it was an accident, it was actually their time to be in spirit."

Through tears, Patricia replied shakily, "We do have faith in God, but we just do not understand why their lives had to end so soon, they were just little boys. What did we do so wrong to deserve this?"

Again, this was not the first time I'd heard this question, but I understood why they might be feeling this way. When a person passes into spirit so young, it is often believed that his or her life was cut short. The truth is that the child's "real life" has actually started earlier, a life we all will share in one day.

I replied to Patricia's comment, "They want you to know you did nothing wrong nor are you being punished by God; God loves both you and also them. They are telling me to let you know that they are smarter than you now and that you just have to trust them when they say that there is a bigger reason for all of this to have happened."

"What could possibly be the reason for this to have happened?" asked Martin.

I replied, "It is not just one reason, but countless, they are telling me. They want you to know their passing into spirit has actually helped more people than you could ever imagine."

At this time, the two boys began pointing at different areas around their body knowing what this would mean to me.

"Did you also donate their organs?" I asked.

"Yes we did. The doctors said that due to the way they passed, their organs were valuable in helping others survive." answered Patricia.

I said. "They want you to know that by doing this, you have helped people in so many ways, ways you can never imagine. They are also saying excitedly that you changed many families' histories!"

"What does that mean?" Martin asked, puzzled.

"You have saved other children's lives, children who now will grow up and have their own families. These lives are only possible through the unselfish act that you and your wife performed by donating their organs. They are saying that this is just one example that may make it easier to understand the reasons for their passing, but that there are numerous others that you do not know. The one thing they do promise you is that one day you will know, just as they do. They are also saying that you taught them to have faith in God so now they are telling you both to do the same as well, and have faith in them."

"I have to be honest, Patrick, I understand, but it really does not make it any easier," Martin said. "I would still rather have them here and if that makes me a selfish person, then so be it."

I replied, "It does not make you a selfish person at all, it only makes you human. The reason you both miss your boys so much is that you love them and there is nothing selfish about that. But by now knowing that Trey and Taylor are still very much alive and with you, you can begin to form a new relationship with them."

"Is that even possible?" Patricia asked.

"It is," I answered. "You have to start not only believing and hoping, but knowing that your sons are still with you; for lack of a better word, they are just invisible now but still your boys. By doing so, you will start to notice more signs around you, and feel their connection with you grow even stronger."

"I do think I feel them around me," Patricia replied.

"That is because you really are with them. These two boys would be hard to miss with their personalities," I confirmed.

Patricia asked, "But how long can they stay with us?"

"What do you mean?" I asked.

Patricia's eyes began to tear up again and she said, "I heard that spirits can only stay around for a short time before they need to move on."

"That is not true," I stated. "There is no such thing as 'moving on'—that is the biggest misconception people have about their loved ones in spirit. Spirits do not have to make a choice of either being here or being in Heaven; they actually get to do both! I can promise you that your wonderful boys are and will be with you, loving you and guiding you both your entire lives."

Both Martin and Patricia started to smile when hearing that, but at the same time, I felt both boys becoming more aggressive with the next message they wanted to get across.

I said, "Trey and Taylor are both laughing and want me to get on you both to stop asking one of your mothers to watch over them. They keep saying that their grandma will not leave them alone!"

Martin, now grinning, replied, "My mother passed away about six months before they did. She always doted on them and so I asked her to keep an eye on them."

"Well, she is!" I said. "And they are both showing me their hair being tousled, what does that mean?"

Martin started laughing. "My mother would always rub their heads and mess up their hair."

"I love it!" I replied.

After more messages from their sons came through along with Martin's mother also joining in the conversation, I could see by the end of the reading that some of the weight of their grief had been lifted.

———

Again, I truly sympathize with anyone having to go through something like this in life, even though there are greater reasons for such tragedies to occur. This is why I feel truly grateful and blessed when I am able to help those in need by showing them the next step in their healing process. And even though I know life will never be the same as it was before they suffered such a loss, I know that it can in fact get better by recognizing that their loved ones in spirit not only continue to live, but also continue to be a part of their lives forever.

6: Being Me

People today are becoming more and more aware of the fact that not only is there an afterlife but also that some people in this world are able to communicate with those who are there, myself being one of them.

Even though I have always had the gift of communicating with those on the other side, I still had to make the decision of whether or not to take it as a profession. In doing so, I knew I was going to enter into a world that already had a certain, how should I say, "reputation" associated with it, one that I was not personally in line with. So I told myself that if I was going to become a medium, even though my main goal in life was going to be helping people understand that there is an afterlife and that their loved ones remain with them always, I also wanted to change people's ideas and any preconceived notions or perceptions as to what a medium really is, or at least to who I really am, anyway.

For example, my physical appearance is certainly different than any other medium out there. Being that I am over six feet, five inches tall, people who meet me for the first time are usually quite surprised by my height. The running joke I tell people is that I am able to communicate with Heaven because I am just a little closer to it than they are. (Not sure how that joke comes across when you're reading it, but it always gets a good laugh when I tell it … I think so anyway …)

Then there is my apparel. To be honest, I am not one who normally wears a suit and tie. When I am on television or just out in public, I am usually more into dressing fashionably casual, going with a leather jacket, jeans, and wearing an earring. And this may even come as a shock to some of you, but I have tattoos! Yes, a medium with tattoos—who knew? And there is also a running joke that you will never see my hair the same way in any two pictures as I am always coloring it or cutting it one way or another.

Also, there is my personality. Even though you may have a feel for it by reading my books or seeing me on television, a lot of people are quite surprised that I not only have a "sixth sense," but I am told that I have a great "sense of humor" as well. Even though I deal with death and dying every day, I still try to make people laugh and smile. (As the saying goes, "Laughter through tears is a great experience.")

And then what sets me apart from other mediums is my belief system. People are often surprised that, as a medium, I am not really into the whole New Age scene—not that there's anything wrong with it—it's just not my style. Also I am not one who uses terms or phrases such as Astral Bodies, Cosmic Consciousness, or even calls myself an Indigo Child. There is enough in this world to learn from, improve, and help with without worrying about "out of this world" fixations.

As a medium, I've had many people tell me that I have in fact helped to break a lot of the stereotypes that are associated with the profession, and I have to tell you that I wear that as a badge of honor. I have given countless interviews to newspapers and on radio and television, each time just being myself. Many times, the interviewer will have had a preconceived notion as to who I am and they are usually surprised to find something or someone they were not anticipating.

Don't get me wrong, there are those out there who do fit more in line with the stereotypical idea of what mediums are and there is nothing wrong with that.

The bottom line is, just like with anything else … mediums too can come in all shapes, sizes, and beliefs. I am just grateful that I am able to do what it is that I do … *while still being able to be me.*

Part 2
The Afterlife

This section is meant to give you a foundation of what I have come to understand about the afterlife from my many years as a medium…the parts we as humans can comprehend, anyway.

Understand that we are spirit first; we are born into this physical realm to learn and to grow from our experiences in this life. Once we have completed this, we then pass into spirit.

When we pass over into spirit, we all go to the other side, which is actually the place we began. It is a physical, solid place, one that is not separate from us, as this physical world we live in actually becomes an extension of it…only separated by a different dimension.

And once we are back in spirit, we continue to oversee and participate with our loved ones and their lives in this physical world as well as continuing to live and to grow in Heaven with God.

7: Body & Soul

Your body is actually made up of two parts, the physical body that you see and the physical soul that you do not, both working in unison with each other... making a whole. Your soul is just as tangible as your physical body, but goes undetected due to the limitations of the five senses that your physical body uses.

Now you may be thinking, how could this be?

Think of it this way: say for some reason you did not have the "sense" of smell. If you went up to a fragrant flower like a rose, you would not be able to detect a smell coming from it as you would lack this sense, even though the scent does exist. The same holds true for your soul. Just because a person is unable to detect that they have a soul does not mean that one doesn't exist.

So when a person passes into spirit, it is only their physical body that dies, not their soul.

When the process of passing over to the other side begins for a person, this is when the soul will start its transition into becoming the dominant part of being. It is also at this point that the soul begins to detach from the body and is why it is referred to as "passing into spirit." And as this transitioning from body to soul occurs, the new physical dimension begins to open up and become apparent … and that dimension is what we refer to as "Heaven." Of course this transition can take place in a split second or much longer, depending on the circumstances of a person's passing.

Once in spirit, your body is in perfect health as it is only the physical body that can be unhealthy, not the soul. There are no illnesses or disabilities in spirit so anyone who may have a handicap or disease in this life will be whole and well in Heaven.

Also, your spirit body does look the same as the physical body as you have now, as it will be in its purest form. Since the physics are different in Heaven, spirits are able to change anything about their bodies they were not happy or not pleased with here. The old can become young, obese can become thin, tall to short, short to tall … the list can go on and on.

———

At one of my demonstrations held in Los Angeles, California, I gave a reading to a family that was sitting in the front row. They were four sisters seemingly close in age, and what I took to be the youngest one was chosen to receive the reading.

"I have your husband here and he is so happy to have the chance to speak with you," I said. The sisters all held hands and seemed excited to be having this experience.

I continued, "He is telling me that you have been missing him."

She started to tear up and nod her head yes. The sister closest to her squeezed her hand for support.

"He passed over recently, didn't he?" I asked.

She answered, "Yes, very recently."

"He is telling me that he would have been in the car with you on the way here tonight but all of you rode together so there was no room for him and besides, he wouldn't get a word in edgewise," I told them.

All the sisters laughed at what he had said because they reported that this was something he would joke about when they were all together. The audience in attendance laughed out loud as well.

His wife asked me, with concern in her eyes, "Is he happy?"

I replied, "He is telling me yes because he is still able to be with his love … that being you."

Tears began to stream down her cheeks.

One of her sisters then started asking questions. "What is he doing? What does he look like?"

Before she could finish her barrage of questions, her sister's husband broke in and started speaking to her so I put my hand up to let her know that he had something to say.

"He is laughing and telling me that it is typical of you to be asking so many questions!" I said.

She replied happily, "Well, he's got that right!"

All the sisters nodded their head in agreement, now beaming.

"He wants you to know that he is still fat and bald and very happy to be so … because that is just who he is!"

With that they all laughed out loud and his wife said she was happy to hear this because she would not want him to ever change!

———

Even though spirits are able to alter their physical appearance in Heaven, you might be surprised by how many of them actually do not. Certainly someone who was perhaps missing an arm or leg or even had some physical disfigurement will change this about themselves, but in Heaven you see what is inside of a person as well as the outside, and that is considered the true beauty of a being in Heaven.

———

Also an individual's personality will usually remain the same, barring any type of mental problems or self-caused affliction one may have had in this life. When giving a reading, I have been told that a spirit's personality will become very apparent by the way I translate the message I am receiving from them. Most of the time I am not aware this is occurring as I am fully concentrating on what the spirit is telling me and then repeating what I am hearing, as well as the way I am hearing it, and this really can highlight a spirit's personality …

When I am connecting with spirits, I do find the majority of them are happy, loving, and positive. These are not only people who have passed of natural causes, but also those who were victims of what are considered unnatural passings, such as accidents and even murders. These souls recognize that there is a greater purpose with theirs or anyone's passing, and this is something that those connected with them can learn and benefit from.

But even though most spirits are happy, this is not always the case...

I recently spoke with a woman named Tammy who wanted to make a connection with her friend John who had been murdered.

John married a sweet girl from the South named Rachel whom he loved dearly. Although Rachel and her family were wonderful people, Rachel had a brother, Scott, who was always in and out of trouble. Scott rarely would come to family gatherings and always wanted something. If he did not get his way, he would usually cause a violent scene. One evening John came home to find Rachel crying. When he asked what was wrong, she said that her brother was on a rampage and she was afraid for Scott's wife, Susan. Scott had mistreated Susan many times in the past when he was in a fit of rage and Rachel did not know what he was going to do to her that night. John, fed up with his brother-in-law, decided to take matters into his own hands and drove over to Scott's house.

Minutes after John entered the house, Scott shot both John and Susan to death.

When I made my connection with John, I could sense from the start that he seemed to be very guarded with the way he used his words and conveyed his feelings. Knowing that I am not only able to hear him, but to also feel his emotions, I could sense that John was frustrated with his current situation.

When I connect with spirits, they will first want their loved ones to know that they are safe, sound, and still very much alive, and they continue to be a part of this life alongside their family and friends. This even held true with John. But when it came to questioning his thoughts and experiences about his passing, I sensed he had a stern countenance, not at all common with spirits.

John first wanted Tammy to know that he was not afraid at all at the time of his passing, and I could sense this was true. He asked Tammy to please tell his wife Rachel that what he did that night was the right thing to do and if he had to do it all over again he would. I was taken aback by the way he was delivering this message because even though some spirits can be very direct when giving messages, John seemed to be extremely straightforward with this one. When I told Tammy what John was relaying, I could not help but also add my thoughts about his directness and the non-emotional way he was communicating. Tammy smiled as her eyes welled up with tears and said that this was no surprise to her, it was just John's way.

As the reading continued, John relayed to Tammy that even though he understood the greater reasoning for what had taken place, he still could not help but be disturbed by his family having to go through the tribulations of the trial and all that was associated with his killer being behind bars. But John wanted his family to know that he was still looking after them and that their safety and their wellbeing were, as always, his number one priorities, even in spirit.

Both Tammy and I could tell by John's words how much he loved his family, even though he was still upset.

After further conversation and the session coming to an end, John again thanked Tammy for setting up the reading, but as Tammy was replying that she was happy to do so, suddenly another spirit approached to speak with me. It was Susan, Scott's wife, who was also murdered.

As I made my connection with Susan to see what she had to say, the feeling from her was completely different from that of John's; her energy was much lighter and more positive. Even though both she and John experienced the same passing at the same time, she seemed to be much more content with what had taken place, which is the norm among most spirits I speak with who have passed under such circumstances.

Susan wanted Tammy to please let Rachel know how sorry she was for what had taken place, and that no matter what happened in the court system with her husband, when Scott made it to the other side… "she was going to kill him."

We both could not help but to laugh at that one.

Tammy was grateful for her messages from both John and Susan. She thanked me for the reading and knew that their messages would in fact help to bring healing to John's family.

———

Again, it is extremely uncommon for me to feel such emotions from a spirit as they know the greater good that can come from any tragic situation. But even in spirit, a person will remain as they were in this physical life (but in their purest, healthiest form) as we are who we are, here or in Heaven, and stubborn people can go to Heaven too ...

8: Spirits Watching Over Us

Most people do in fact believe in an afterlife and so it is also a common hope that their loved ones in spirit are watching over them in Heaven.

Would you be surprised if I were to tell you that this is one of the biggest misconceptions people have about their loved ones in spirit?

The truth is that your loved ones in spirit are not only in Heaven watching you, but still continue to participate with you in this life as well! There is no separation from spirits from this physical realm ... as this world is essentially also a part of Heaven.

Though this may be hard to comprehend, try thinking of it this way:

Reading this book, you see that there are words written on one side of a page. When you are finished reading one side, you will flip the page over and see that there are more words on the other side of the page.

Even though both sides of a page contain words, each side of the page is seemingly separate from the other.

But wait, what if you were to hold a page up to a light. What would happen?

You would see that the illumination would reveal all the words on the front and back side of the paper intertwining with each other at the same time.

And this is how it is with Earth and Heaven.

You can say that we are on one side of the page in this physical life and spirits are on the other side of the page living their spirit life, with both sides coexisting on the same piece of paper—one side Earth, the other side Heaven. But just as with the above example, most people living in this physical plane are unaware of what is on the other side of the page. By the light of God, those on the other side in spirit are able to see and experience both sides, their world as well as ours.

By spirits being able to experience both worlds, both realities, your loved ones in spirit are able continue to be a part of your life here on Earth. By this I mean they not only watch you and observe what you do in your life, but will actually help you by guiding you down certain paths that will help in the growth of your soul. There are many ways your loved ones in spirit help guide you in this life, and though most are in ways you can never imagine, there are a few that you are able to understand.

Do you have a "gut instinct"?

This is a term used to describe a feeling you have sometimes in the pit of your stomach that directs you to do something. But what is it really?

It's an odd concept, if you think about it, why would your "gut" have an instinct in the first place? Does your appendix have an instinct? How about your left toe, what is it telling you to do today? See my point? Even though the truth is that your "gut" does not really have an instinct, there is something that does takes place down there.

That sensation you have experienced from time to time deep inside your stomach can be your own intuitive/psychic ability coming through, but most of the time it is actually a loved one in spirit guiding you into doing what you should be doing!

Spirits will give you that "feeling" of something being right or something being wrong, and by doing so, will help guide you with decisions you are facing. But what happens sometimes is that "gut" tells you to do one thing and your "brain" tells you to do another, and this is where you can run into problems.

I remember Kathy being at a store one time and on the counter were various "impulse" items that stores place near the registers. When she was just about to pay for the items she was purchasing, she glanced over and saw a can of air that fixes flat tires. For whatever reason, something in her gut was telling her to buy it, and at first she resisted. She thought to herself that she had seen the product a thousand times before so why buy it now? But she kept experiencing a "nagging" feeling so she gave in and purchased the can of tire fix.

When Kathy got back to her car, she tossed the can of air in the trunk and went on her way. About a week later, after shopping at a mall one evening, Kathy discovered that her car had a flat tire! At first Kathy became worried, as not only was she all alone late at night in a parking garage, but was also unsure of the condition of the spare tire, which she had never used. Then suddenly relieved, Kathy remembered she had, in fact, given in to her gut instinct and purchased the can of air to fix the tire. It took her only a matter of minutes to inflate her tire and she was on her way, safe and sound, happy that she'd acted on her gut instinct.

Remember, it can be big life-changing decisions or small, everyday occurrences that your loved ones in spirit help you with, but always listen to what your gut is telling you, as your gut/loved ones in spirit are never wrong!

———

Another way spirits will help guide you is by your simply hearing them. What, you don't think you hear your loved ones in spirit? Don't be surprised when I tell you that you hear from them all the time and by this I mean … through your thoughts!

Have you ever wondered where that good idea came from that you had or why you had the voice inside your head telling you to do something or not to do something? This is actually a loved one in spirit communicating with you telepathically. Though you may not hear their voices exactly, you will hear thoughts they are giving you that can help guide you, or they will let you know they love you and are with you.

Have you ever been struggling with a perplexing question such as what is wrong with the car or what ingredient is missing from a recipe when suddenly it pops into your head? This is usually help from your loved ones.

I hear all the time from people saying they believe that they hear their loved ones in spirit in their head. When they tell me this, they always ask me if I think they are crazy. I usually laugh and reply that I speak to dead people for a living and they are asking me if I think they are the crazy ones?

But I tell them that I don't think they are crazy as it happens to people all the time. I'll bet many of you right now are agreeing that this has happened to you!

As I mentioned earlier, it does not even have to be a voice that you hear, but perhaps just a thought. Spirits will place thoughts in your head, as well, as a way to give you a foundation of truth or ideas you can build on.

Now, of course, you may be wondering if loved ones in spirit are watching out for you, then why is it that problems still arise?

It is actually not that difficult to understand. Again, you are in this physical life in order for your soul to grow. This development only happens through experiencing the occurrences and situations you encounter in your life … good and bad. And believe it or not, it is usually the difficult challenges in life that give you the most opportunity for your soul's growth.

But remember, even though there are certain things spirits are able to help you with in this life, you always have the choice to listen to them or not.

So if you think that your loved ones in spirit are away from you or just standing around and watching you live your life, think again. Even though there may be a thin veil between you and your loved ones who have passed, once in spirit, that veil is completely removed and spirits not only are able to enjoy all that Heaven is, but they also continue loving you and participating in this life with you as well.

You can say they get the best of both worlds…

9: God, Heaven & Hell

This section is the hardest part of the book for me to write as how do you describe something we are incapable of fathoming?

So let's just start off with the biggest question of all:

Is there a God? The answer is positively yes, there is a God.

But if you are imagining God as an old man who walks around in some great kingdom beyond the clouds and sits on a throne to judge people … think again.

Anytime I talk about God when I am communicating with spirits, the one definitive answer that they tell me is that they are in the "Presence of God." But they also express to me there are no words, descriptions, or images they could communicate to me that would ever come close to actually describing God.

God is simply beyond what our human minds can grasp or comprehend.

Now you may be asking why they are unable to put into words or images who or what God really is if they themselves are experiencing God and are in his presence?

I too thought the same, and I was once speaking with a spirit and asked him this question. This spirit then proceeded to give me a perfect example of why they are unable to do so. This spirit asked me a question, which was, "How would you describe the color green to a blind person? You see it and experience it and by doing so, you know that it is real. But how would you relay the color green in words to someone who is deprived of sight? It would be impossible as there are no words that could truly describe it."

And with that simple example, I understood why they were unable to tell me exactly who or what God is as there are no words to describe him.

We live in a physical world where most people have and use five senses… well, really more, but we will get into that later. In spirit, people gain more than just the five senses that people use here, and with these added senses, they are able to understand and comprehend who and what God is in Heaven.

Personally, I always refer to God as a he or him just out of habit, but I know that God goes far beyond a he, a she, or of anything we can ever conceive.

So when it comes to trying to picture who or what God really is, I stopped trying a long time ago. Why try to solve an unsolvable puzzle? God is real, God is an intelligent presence, God is the creator of all, and we are all a part of God. For me, that is good enough for now as I know that I, too, along with everyone else in this world, will one day have the answer to that question.

———

Okay, so you now may be asking yourself, if there is a God, then there must be a Heaven … right?

The answer to your question is yes, of course there is. Where else would spirits and God live?

Now even though we are unable to really grasp who or what God is, we are in fact able to have more of an understanding of what Heaven is like, but in a very small, limited way. And even though there are many things in Heaven that go far beyond what we can comprehend or could ever imagine, there are things there that are in fact very similar to what we know and experience here in this life.

First, Heaven is a physical place.

Everything that is positive about this physical world is also in Heaven. Birds, trees, animals, lakes, and oceans, pretty much all we physically have here on Earth we too can experience in Heaven. Let us just say that God has given everyone on this Earth only a preview of things to come.

And not only are the physical things we experience here a part of Heaven, but so also is any activity we enjoy doing—socializing, entertaining, and sporting events, for instance. People in spirit can still enjoy such things in Heaven, as well as continue to enjoy participating in them here.

———

I gave a reading on air to a radio listener one time and she asked for me to speak with her father.

"Your father is telling me that you are very much like him. He says that you like to keep busy as well as plan everything ahead of time," I said.

She replied, "Very much so, this reading is just the start of a very busy day!"

"He wants you to know that he too has a busy day ahead of him." I said.

I thought this message was strange as spirits usually talk more about what they do for their loved ones here, not what their plans are for the day. Nevertheless, I continued.

"He says after speaking with you, he is going to play a round of golf with some of his spirit friends."

This made her laugh. "I was wondering if he was still able to do that!"

"And after that, he says he is planning on taking your mother out to dinner."

She chuckled. "Ask him who's paying for it."

"He says he heard that! And to answer your question, he said tonight it is his treat."

"Tell him to have a good time and not be cheap with the tip."

I started laughing at that one. "He never is, he says."

This reading was to me a great example of how spirits can and will continue to do the things that they enjoyed here as well. And if you think about it, why would it be so hard to believe that Heaven has similar activities to those on Earth? If you trust that God is the one who created the Earth and was the one who put you here in the first place, then why would he place you in a location that is of a different nature and physicality to where you would end up going?

Sure, this world certainly has its faults. But I am sure you would agree that behind all the challenges and negativities that people may experience here, Earth can actually be a pretty heavenly place!

———

So if there is a God and also a Heaven, are there such things as angels?

The answer is yes. But just as with countless other truths about Heaven, they too go beyond what we can imagine.

Angels are defined as messengers of God in the Hebrew Bible—the Torah—the New Testament, and the Quran. The term "angel" has also been expanded to various notions of "spiritual beings" found in many other religious traditions. Roles of angels include protecting and guiding human beings.

I remember I was once giving a reading to my sister Kathy when suddenly I felt a higher energy unexpectedly make a connection with me. It really is difficult to describe, but I can only say that it was a faster and lighter "being" full of immense love.

Unbeknownst to me, Kathy had seen a story on television the night before about a young girl who had been in a coma for many years. Many people knew of this girl and would visit her bedside to say prayers for her.

People also came to her bedside to pray for miracles for themselves and loved ones in need. Kathy is highly sensitive to people's feelings and she told me that the story touched her heart so much to see that young girl, who lay motionless as many, many people brought their sufferings to her, yet she interceded that they might have relief. How amazed she was by that little angel in the bed. Kathy later told me that it was so hard for her to stop crying after that story. Feeling such compassion for that young girl, Kathy prayed to the Blessed Mother as hard as she could that night to comfort the child who brought comfort to so many.

While I was giving Kathy the reading she certainly did not expect this to come up. We were talking to our loved ones in spirit and then that, shall I say, angelic energy came to me. The message was that the Blessed Mother Mary had heard Kathy's heartfelt prayer and felt the love that she shared for that child.

It was wonderful to experience that level of higher energy and love for us both.

———

So how do you think you would act if you were ever to encounter an angel here on Earth?

Let's say one day you were strolling along and suddenly a beautiful angel with magnificent wings, surrounded by a brilliant glowing loving light appeared before you. Faced with this glorious being in all of its glory and reverence, what would you do? How would you act toward this angel? If I were to guess, I would bet many of you would drop to your knees and feel blessed by the miracle of being in such a presence.

But what if I were to tell you that you have probably already encountered an angel in your life and that you probably did not act like that or in fact even realize that you had seen one?

Even though angels are magnificent winged beings who help and guide people from Heaven, they also come into this physical world to provide people with even more opportunities for soul growth. But when they are on this physical plane, they can take a shape that is quite the opposite of what you would think an angel should have.

- An angel can be the homeless man you see on the street.
- An angel can be the alcoholic staggering out of the liquor store.
- An angel can be the old man sitting with his head hanging down all alone on the park bench with no one to talk to.
- An angel can be the lady in front of you in line at the store who is low on money and has to put groceries back.
- Angels can come in all shapes and sizes.

———

My father and mother were young sweethearts before they got married. They knew they were both meant for one another and my father even had a ring and a marriage license ready for when that special day of marriage was going to take place.

So on a cold December evening, being the romantics that my father and mother were, they decided that they could not wait any longer and had to get married that night.

Since it was late on this particular winter evening, the temperature had become bitterly cold, dropping well below zero, with snow still covering the ground, left behind from a storm they'd had the night before.

As late as it was, with the inclement weather, traveling down the roads that evening was eerily lonely as no other cars were in sight. They were both anxious to get married and, wanting to get to the church as quickly as they could, my father decided to take a short cut and headed down a dark, deserted road. About a mile or so down this road they came across a set of barricades blocking their way. My father knew there was construction going on in that area for new housing and just figured that they were set up as parameters for the construction workers. So he drove around the barricades and they continued on in their quest.

As my parents resumed driving on the long snowy desolate road, they noticed a small light swinging from side to side up in the distance. As they drew closer they became aware that it was a little old man who was swinging a lantern to get their attention. My father stopped the car when they reached the man as they both thought he might need assistance. Why else would anyone be out in this cold, almost unbearable wind, my father thought. The man was bundled up and the wind howled as my father rolled down his window. Keep in mind that my father was a popular man about town and knew just about everyone, but he did not recognize this man with the lantern.

The man greeted my parents with a smile and they asked him if he needed help. He laughed and told them they were the ones who needed his help. Confused, my father asked him what he meant. This man told my parents that the road up ahead was under construction and if they had kept going, the car would have ended up dropping off a twenty- or thirty-foot precipice!

Both my mom and dad were extremely grateful to say the least and thanked the man for the warning. He wished my parents well and told them to stay warm, waving to them as they turned around and headed back.

Looking back in the rearview mirror, my father noticed that the man was no longer there.

As they continued to drive and discussing what had almost taken place, they both started to wonder why this old man would be standing outside in the middle of nowhere with a lantern in the late hours of the night. He had no car, nor were there any houses for miles. And it was so cold that night, it would be impossible for anyone to be out in it for any reasonable length of time.

Without saying any words, they looked at each other and smiled, realizing that Heaven may have just lent a helping hand to them.

If this man had not stopped my parents on that dark and lonely road that snowy night, their car would had probably driven off the steep embankment and they would not have survived.

They did get married that night and had a long happy life thanks to the angel on that winter's eve.

So you may want to think twice next time before passing a person on the street who may need help or is offering help as it could be someone working on God's behalf... for yours!

———

So if there is a Heaven, is there a Hell and do bad people go there?

The answer to that is yes and no.

Many people think of "Hell" as a physical place where the devil lives amongst sulfuric smoldering pits and where a soul is condemned by God for all of eternity if a sinner. Some religions teach that if you do not believe in their God, their values, and only their religion, then your soul will burn in Hell. So if that really were the case, there in fact would be billions and billions of people in Hell, including children.

So you have to ask yourself, would a loving God really put so many people, even children, in a place such as Hell? No, he would not and to believe otherwise is just ridiculous.

If you think about it, if God is all-loving and will forgive you of all of your sins here on Earth before you pass, then why wouldn't he also forgive you of your sins after you pass into spirit?

God forgives people of their sins no matter where they are, here or in spirit.

But the truth is that there is what you might call a "Hell" on the other side, but it is not in a separate location or even an actual place at all. Hell is not a noun, but an adjective as it is essentially a state of being on the other side.

Unlike what some religions preach, God is not the one who punishes you on the other side for any of your negative or wrong deeds or actions on Earth, it is essentially "you" who punishes yourself. Even Blessed Pope John Paul II said before his passing, "Think of Hell as a state of mind, a self-willed exile from God."

When you pass over into spirit, it is the realization of your own thoughts and deeds that you had experienced here that will lead you to whatever level you will exist in on the other side. Again, do not think of these levels as an actual physical place, being up or down, here or there. These levels are ones of consciousness … a consciousness of who you really are. It is similar to the way we all live on Earth; even though we all live on the same planet, we all experience this life in our own unique way. And once in spirit, you have pure thoughts and insights on how you lived your life here and how you affected others. You understand what the purpose of your life was and reflect on how well you lived it. There, you see the opportunities you were given. Which ones you grew from but also which ones you missed out on.

On the other side, those who are in a Hell state are people who caused harm to others. Do not get me wrong, no one is perfect on this Earth and we all act in ways we regret. But these are souls who have mistreated people physically or even psychologically and had little to no regret or remorse in doing so. And with this, these souls experience and endure the cause and effects of their actions from that life.

Usually when I connect with spirits, their vibrations are at a fast and light pace. This is challenging to explain, but it is similar to how you may feel when you are really excited. When I connect with people who are at a lower level, their vibration is slower, and it comes with an emotion of sadness surrounding them.

———

Not so long ago I spoke with someone who came to me who was in this state of being.

"I have your husband here and the first thing I am feeling from him is sadness." I said.

This is usually not the case when I connect with most spirits, so I knew her husband must have done something really wrong in his life. His wife started to cry.

I continued. "I'm getting the sense from your husband that he was not a very nice guy."

She began to cry harder as she clutched a tissue tightly in her hand. "You can say that again. I knew he was a pretty bad person, I just did not realize how bad he was going to become," she replied.

"There were times of physical abuse to you, he is telling me," I relayed.

She put her head down and replied, "Many times."

I patted her hand and continued. "He is also telling me that you were not the only person he hurt."

"This is very true," she replied as the tears came down her face.

"Your husband is showing me a gun and said he used it on someone."

"He killed someone over money," she said.

"He wants you to know more than anything how truly sorry he is for what he has done."

The sad expression on her face lifted a bit as it seemed it had been those words she was waiting to hear from him.

I could tell this spirit was genuinely sorry for his actions and so glad to have the opportunity to try to set things right.

"He is telling me that he knows it is going to take some time, but he is hoping to one day have your and others' forgiveness. There are things that you know about him, but many things you do not. And he wants you to know that he is now paying for the way he lived his life here. In his case, there were no excuses for the way he lived, just that he only thought of himself with everything he did and the way he lived."

"Even though I do not want anything to do with him any longer, I do hope he is getting the help he needs," she responded with a compassionate look on her face.

"Believe it or not, part of the help he needs is in fact your forgiveness—it not only will help him, but more importantly it will help you as well."

"I will try. It may take some time, but I will try."

"That is all he can ask for, he is telling me."

———

Everyone going through this life has done minor things that have hurt someone else. These are actions we regret and perhaps from which we even learned a lesson. We learn and grow from conflict in our lives. But there are things some people do that go beyond everyday negatives such as killing, abuse, and so on. People who commit such acts are the ones who are in a Hell state, that is, if they were as "clear of mind" as the man above.

There are times when such crimes and negative acts have been caused by someone who was not in their right state of mind, people who perhaps were under the influence of drugs, alcohol, or even who were mentally abused or mentally ill. These types usually are not in that Hell state as they had no control over their actions. But with these occurrences, there are lessons from which both a person and spirit will learn.

Keep in mind that anyone who is in a Hell state does not stay there forever … the length of time is up to them. They too can still learn and grow from their mistakes, and these souls can even reincarnate and hopefully continue their spiritual growth by reliving another life here on Earth where they can continue to grow in spirit.

Again, God is the epitome of love and does not judge us in the afterlife—we judge ourselves. On the other side, after we see and, yes, feel what we have caused others, we can be harder on ourselves than anyone else … even God.

———

So you may now be wondering, if Hell is just a state of mind, is there a devil?

No, there is no devil.

The belief that the devil is a fallen angel from God and that he is the cause of all evil here on Earth sounds to me as if man is trying to push the blame for his own bad deeds off onto someone or something else. And why would man have the need to do this? Because throughout the history of time, it has been the easiest way for people to explain away negative things or why people commit terrible acts.

One time Kathy and I were watching our five-year-old nephew, Connor. Though usually a good boy, this particular day he was acting up quite a bit and not doing what he was being told to do. This was unusual for his character so I asked him why he was behaving badly. His response was, "the devil is on my shoulder!"

This took me by surprise and I asked him why he would say that. Connor told me that someone told him when children misbehave in this way they have the devil on their shoulders. I could not believe that he was told that and said to him that there was no devil and that he was just acting badly! Funny, however, after he received that message, he was good for the rest of the day.

There really was no devil making my nephew act this way, just a five-year-old boy flexing his "what can I get away with" muscle!

This is a simple example of how people can justify their bad behavior by blaming it on something that does not exist. And if you think about it, if a devil was the one who made a person do bad things, would that imply that angels are the ones making a person do good things? And if this were the case, it would be as if humans had no judgment or free will and we were just being controlled by good and bad spirits.

If you try to process this logically … if there was some type of evil devil running around causing harm to people, why wouldn't our loving God just do away with him? He was the one that supposedly created him in the first place, right?

Remember, the negative things that you encounter here in this world are what give your soul the opportunity to learn and to grow. And that certainly would not be the job of any devil.

10: RELIGION

They say the two things you should never discuss with friends are religion and politics. Well, I will keep my politics to myself, but let's do talk religion.

Would you be surprised if I told you that God is not religious?

Now at this point, you may be shouting, "What, God is not religious! What are you talking about, Patrick?" Just please keep reading…

The dictionary defines religion as: a specific fundamental set of beliefs and practices generally agreed upon by a number of persons or sects: the Christian religion; the Buddhist religion; the list is endless.

So if you think about it, if God was religious, it would mean that he would be believing in and worshipping himself. Why would he do this?

Religions stem from the writings of men and prophets relaying stories of holy experiences and inspirations.

These writings have been scribed, transcribed, and rewritten many times throughout history. And though some of these writings may have been inspired by God, these writings have also been greatly influenced by man's misguidance, politics, and the biases of their times. This is why there are so many contradictions found in these writings.

There are many different forms of religions in this world, and the ones that have the foundation of believing there is a God and an afterlife have it right. (I think we all can agree with that.) Where the problems begin is when any one religion teaches that theirs is the real and only true religion and that their teachings are the only way to God and Heaven.

This is where man's ignorance, prejudice, and scare tactics come into play, which has nothing at all to do with God.

Any religion that helps to bring you closer to God's love and a love for others is a wonderful religion to follow. What is not so wonderful is if a religion teaches prejudice, injustice, and invokes fear, as these intolerances have nothing at all to do with God. God is all-loving and does not invoke fear in anyone in order to force them to believe in him. So why is it that some religions incite such fear in their followers? The reason is because many people are led by fear, and man, knowing this, takes advantage of these people by causing them to fear God.

———

Kathy and I used to have some friends with whom we would argue … oops, I mean discuss this. Their belief was that no matter how good a person is, if he or she doesn't believe in Jesus, that person could not enter Heaven.

That sure does leave a lot of people standing outside those Heavenly gates, doesn't it?

We would ask them, how about those who were unaware of Jesus?

–No Heaven.

How about those of other faiths?

–No Heaven.

Those who did not believe in God?

–No Heaven

Those who were not saved?

–No Heaven

The list went on and on.

So we would ask them: are they telling us that it did not make any difference if someone lived a good life, was helpful to others and believed in God, just not Jesus? That not only was that person not going to Heaven, he or she was going to spend eternity in Hell with the devil?

Their answer: yes!

Really … really???

And if you asked them why this was true, their answer would be because their religion told them so. No real rational reason, just because their religion dictated it.

This is when a religion can take a normal, rational, smart person and strip away their ability to use common sense. Again, think about it. Why would God be angry at someone who lives their life "Christ"-like, but just does not believe in Jesus, and condemn their soul to an eternal Hell? How does that make any sense?

It does not.

By the way, one of them is no longer our friend as he also decided that he disagreed with the work that Kathy and I do ... all due to his religious beliefs.

It is sad when a religion can ruin a friendship ...

———

If you do follow a religion, whatever religion, it should bring you the comfort of God's love and help to make you a better person. BUT it should also help you to be respectful of other people's beliefs as well.

Always remember that religion can be a good thing if used as a tool to heighten your soul's awareness of truth and love. But it can also be a bad thing if used as a weapon.

So is there religion in Heaven?

Sure there is, and you can still continue with the same one that you practiced here, but let's just say it is somewhat tweaked.

In Heaven you no longer use religion to help you to "believe" in God, as over there his existence becomes unquestionable. Religion on the other side is used more for praising God and celebrating everything that he has created.

Sometimes I am asked what religion or church do I follow. Though I was raised a Catholic, I personally do not follow any religion or go to any church now as I consider myself spiritual. And my definition of spiritual is knowing there is a God, knowing there is an afterlife, and knowing my loved ones in spirit are helping me in this life, along with trying to be the best person I can be.

Because, as the saying goes, God is too big for just one religion.

11: Atheists Go to Heaven

If you do not believe in God, will you still go to Heaven?

Of course you will.

If you are a good person, love and help others, and act "Godlike" but do not believe in God, why wouldn't God still love you and want you with him in Heaven?

As discussed earlier, even though everyone actually goes to the same place once a person passes over into spirit, it is how you lived your life here that defines the experience you'll live on the other side.

If you do not believe in God, this does not necessarily make you a bad person, just as the opposite holds true, as there are many immoral people who do believe in God.

One of the benefits of believing in God and perhaps even following a religion is that, by doing so, it can help a person find comfort and perhaps solutions to life's everyday challenges. Believing in God can also help someone connect with their higher self. If you are one who believes in God and Heaven, I am sure you would agree that it does make this world and life here a whole lot easier.

If you are one who does not believe in God and Heaven, your view of this world and life is probably seen more in a black-and-white scenario. More likely, you believe that people are born on Earth because life just happened by chance and when a person dies, that person no longer exists. Personally, I am amazed by those who believe this and still can manage to get out of bed in the morning. I personally cannot imagine living this life not believing, or in my case, "knowing" that my loved ones in spirit are guiding me in this life. But again, this belief of nonbelief does not make you or anyone with the same belief a bad person; you are just minus something of the knowledge in this life that the rest of us are experiencing: God's love and our loved ones in spirit. But as an atheist, you can and will instead experience these things indirectly, such as in spiritual upliftment through passions, for instance as in music, working on hobbies, or being with family and friends, etc. But keep in mind, as with everyone else here on Earth, nonbelievers still have the love and guidance of their loved ones in spirit as well as the love of God … even if they do not believe.

———

I recall a reading where I connected a woman named Ellen with her husband Ben. Ellen was extremely concerned about her husband's spirit as he did not believe in God or an afterlife.

"Ben is here and he's laughing about something," I said to Ellen.

She replied, "He is actually here?"

"Well, of course he is; he says he made it!" I replied.

"Oh, thank God!" she replied.

"Ben is saying thank God is right!" I said. "He wants you to know that you were right about something."

With a big grin on her face, she questioned, "Oh, what is that?"

"I am getting the sense from him that he did not believe in God and wants you to know that you were right … there is a God!"

With that Ellen began to cry happy tears. "I was so praying that he would!"

"He is bragging that, being in spirit now, he knows a lot more about Heaven and God than even you!" I relayed to her.

With that, she laughed harder and replied, "I'll bet he does!"

I continued, "Ben wants you to know that being in spirit, he is now able to see how different his life would have been if he had believed in God and with that, he means that it would have given his life another dimension. But he is in fact proud of the way he lived his life and loved his family and holds no regrets."

"He was always a good man," she agreed proudly.

"He still is, he says. So he wants you to stop worrying and wants me to tell you that the devil is not running around and poking him with a pitchfork!"

Again, this made Ellen laugh out loud.

"I should hope not!"

I added, "And by the way, he wants you to know that he has met the 'Big Man' and he tells you 'Hello'!"

"Oh, God is saying hi to me?" she asked quizzically.

I replied, "No, Ben is not saying God, but 'Elvis' … the other big man."

We laughed together at that one as Ellen and Ben both were, and still are, huge Elvis fans!

It is funny that anytime I have made a connection with someone in spirit who was an atheist here, their first response when arriving on the other side is, "Oops, guess I was wrong!"

So you can say that there is no such thing as an atheist in Heaven because once a person of this belief has passed, they know that God and Heaven do in fact exist.

12: SUICIDES GO TO HEAVEN TOO

A person who commits suicide will see and feel the cause and effect created by the action of taking one's own life. This determines what level that individual will be on once reaching the other side.

There are many reasons why someone may decide to take their own life, and because of this, they can exist at various levels in Heaven. For example, someone who was not in their "right state of mind" due to drugs or alcohol may have taken their own life accidentally. Perhaps this person was fooling around and doing something idiotic that they should not have been doing and ended up dying. On the other side, this person may feel "stupid" for what they have done, but they are actually at a good level in spirit as their passing was in fact simply an accident, and accidents are usually meant to be.

I recently spoke with a father whose son had passed from an accidental drug overdose. I could tell instantly that his son was at a good level of being and that it was in fact an accident. And even though during the reading it came out that his son did not mean to take his own life, the father still did not understand why God would be so cruel as to allow his son to die and cause him go through such pain over the loss.

His son felt so much compassion for his father and told him that, in his case, it was just his time to be in spirit and that there were actually many lessons that had been, or were to be, learned from his passing. He said to his father that even though it did seem as if God was being cruel, in fact he was not, as this was a part of the soul's growth process that his father needed to experience. By going through this, his soul would arrive at a place in life that would not otherwise have been possible. And though the answer was not in front of him at this very moment, he wanted his dad to trust him that one day it would be. And most of all, they both would be learning these life lessons together.

If someone may have had mental issues, or if their mind just snapped in anger, they too would be at a good level in spirit because they were not in control of what they were doing. An example of this would be if there has ever been a time in your life when you were so mad at something or someone that you put your fist through a wall or even broke an inanimate object. This act of violence is not really who you are and does not define you as a person. But just at that one split moment in time, you wanted to react in an aggressive way.

Some people who commit suicide may also have what you might call a slow corrosion of the mind. This could have been caused by depression, drugs—you name it. Although their mind did not snap in an instant as in the above examples, it made them no more responsible for taking their own life, as it was a slow progression of their mind not functioning at a normal level.

Then there are those who knew exactly what they were doing and just felt they did not want to live any longer. Yes, these people still go to the other side as well, but are at what you would consider a lower level. When these spirits connect with me, they have a slower or lower vibration. The only way I can describe it is that your body may feel kind of "weighty" when in an upset or depressed mood. This person usually will come to me very remorseful for their actions because they see that whatever the situation was at the time that caused them to take their life (even if the situation was lasting a day, week, month, or even years), it in fact would have passed. They also see what things they were going to do and could have achieved, but now are unable to do. They also experience the effect their suicide has had on their family and friends.

So do these types of suicides stay in Heaven "forever" regretting what they have done?

There is no time limit on how long a spirit will be at this state as it really is up to the individual how they will continue their soul's progression on the other side.

But forgiveness and love for these spirits from those they left behind can go a long way in helping them with their process of healing.

———

Every person's life here is precious and a gift from God. Even though not everyone will discover a cure for a disease, become a celebrity, or even become financially wealthy, this does not make one's life more or less important than those people who do. We are all sharing this lifetime together for a reason and are actually connected with one another more than could ever be realized.

Your life has an effect on this Earth—and without you here, this world would truly not be the same.

13: The Good Die Young

When someone passes away in their eighties or beyond, it is natural to think they had a good long life and it was just their time. But when a child passes, most people think that their life has been cut short.

Not true.

The soul enters into the physical body in order to learn and to grow from the experiences encountered here on Earth. Once the physical body dies, the same soul will then continue to live on into the next life. Though you may think of it as two different lives, it actually is not—it is just the continuation of the same one. Even if a person passes at a young age, their life in reality has not been cut short at all ... their time in this physical world, yes, but their actual life, no, as being in spirit is when our real life begins.

There are infinite numbers of reasons why children pass into spirit, a few of them being:

- Their souls do not need a full lifespan in this physical dimension in order to learn the lessons intended for them.

- They need to become spirit in order to help with the growth and lessons of others, such as their family members and other loved ones in this physical plane.

- Other people will learn or could even benefit from their passing, such as people in the medical field, or even someone having their life saved from the donation of an organ.

The reasons are endless why someone passes at a young age, but the one thing to remember is that it is never a punishment by God, only an opportunity for soul growth.

———

I recall speaking with a woman named Erin whose son William, Willie for short, had passed at the young age of nine years old due to a heart defect he'd had since birth. Erin came to me with the hope that she could learn if Willie was all right, but she got more than that…

We sat down together and I could see that Erin was anxious to get started. Her high energy was palpable. I could easily tell why her son too was full of energy and eager to start.

"Willie is connecting with me and wow, is he full of life!" I said.

Smiling from ear-to-ear, Erin exclaimed, "My baby!"

"Now this is coming from him, not me, but he is telling me to ask you to stop calling him a baby! But I can tell he doesn't mean it, Erin," I relayed to her.

Erin gasped and replied with her hand over her mouth, "Oh my God, he always told me that! The older he got the more he disliked it."

I could see Willie standing beside his mother giving her a bear hug. "He is hugging you now and wants you to know that he will always be your baby."

As Erin wiped away her tears we continued.

I then said, "Willie is thanking you and is telling me you are still helping him."

Erin had a puzzled look on her face, rubbed her chin and asked, "I am?"

"Yes, he said that you not only took such good care of him when he was here, but you still continue to do so."

Even though I need to concentrate intently on hearing a spirit's message and conveying it, I still also try to understand the meaning of what it is they are trying to express. Willie also had me wondering what he was talking about.

"Willie says that he understands how hard it was for you to help him with his ill health, through the constant care, the hospital visits, and the late nights sitting beside his bed when he could not sleep. He also knows how angry you were after his passing and that this was due to how much you loved him and still love him. And he is very proud that you have taken your pain and turned such a negative into a positive."

"Lord knows I have tried," Erin replied, nodding her head with tears starting to stream down her cheeks. "I am a firm believer in God and I know that William is still with me, I feel him, I truly do. Before my baby … I mean, my little man passed, he made me promise that I would do everything that I could to be happy; he said he was happy when I was happy and smiling and that he would be watching for me to be so again."

Hearing this, I too could not help but start to tear up.

Erin sat up straight in her chair and said, "So after Willie died, I prayed, asking him for strength to take me on my next path."

With this, Willie began to show me a vision.

"Well, he did. Willie is taking you by your hand and leading you down the right path. He is telling me what makes him so joyous is that he did not have to grab your hand and try to pull you down the path, but instead you are walking down it hand-in-hand together. And this is why William is happy."

Erin rubbed her hand as if she could feel his hand in hers. She told me, "After his passing I could either sit around and feel sorry for myself, something I told Willie neither one of us should do, or I could change the situation. I decided to do something positive! I started a blog for parents who are in the same situation where they can learn and draw strength from one another's experiences."

"Well, Willie says proudly that you have been and will be helping more people than you can imagine. He wants to tell you that going through what you did with his illness helped you to learn so much about giving and loving, and he says that you already know that this is what life is all about. Now you are sharing that with so many who need it." I added, "He is so proud of his mama!"

I thought to myself, how selfless for this wonderful woman who has had the greatest loss of her life, the loss of her child, to be able to turn that unimaginable event into a way of helping others.

I could see Erin's eyes sparkle as she smiled. She responded, "I do know this and I believe it. I am just grateful that he is so healthy now and most importantly, still able to be with me."

Hearing his mother's response, Willie started laughing.

"He wants me to tell his mama that he may have had a small weak heart here on Earth but because of the love and care from you, he has the biggest and best in Heaven!"

———

When a child passes, it is natural to think that they did not have a chance to live a full life experience, such as playing with friends, going to school, and growing into their teen years and adulthood, missing out on all of the wonderful opportunities life has to offer. But this is really not the case at all. The truth is that children who pass into spirit actually still experience all of what is available here, along with everything else that Heaven offers.

Children in spirit are never scared or sad about being there, as they understand why they are in spirit and are surrounded by loved ones in spirit as well as by God's love. Children can remain the same age as they were the day they passed, as well as grow year by year as each birthday is celebrated. It really depends on the child and their individual situation. But no matter what age the children are, even though their personalities can still be childlike, their souls are in fact more mature.

So when a child passes into spirit, he or she is actually getting a head start on what the rest of us will one day be a part of—Heaven. (And from what I have been told, it is not a bad place to be!)

14: Passing into Spirit

So what is the experience really like when someone dies?

I am not sure if you have noticed, but in this book, I try not to use the words "die" or "dying." Why? Because the word "die" has such a harsh connotation, a finality to it, and the fact is, people do not actually die. A person's body dies, yes; their souls, no. And it is only an illusion that we are our body, when in fact we are our soul.

First, there is a misconception that death is painful, and this is not the case.

You have to remember that a person dies because of something that has taken place within their physical body. Whatever the reason for the death, that is what the person will experience pain from, not the actual death itself.

When someone is crossing over, the transition is like no other experience that a human has ever had in their life. There is absolutely no pain associated with it, in fact it is quite the opposite, it is a great relief. Once a person is in spirit, they are completely free of any pain or disabilities they may have been coping with during their life as well as during their passing.

You see, everything experienced in this physical body is limited to what senses we possess and with that we gauge the positive and negative physical experiences we have on Earth. Once a spirit releases from its body, not only do the five senses continue to exist with the soul, but additional senses become awakened as well, ones we cannot fathom.

As a spirit, a person is free of any physical negative sensations that their body needed to have in order to help them to gain soul growth while living in this world, meaning they are of pure physical health. The reason I use the word physical is that a soul is in fact still very much a physical being, only one that exists in another dimension—Heaven.

Though each passing is a different experience for every person, there are some common factors during a person's transition to spirit.

What usually takes place once a person passes into spirit is similar to when you awaken in the morning. Sometimes you will instantly wake up and know what time and day it is. But then there are times when you wake up and it takes you a minute or so to shake off the sleep and become fully awake … and it is the same with spirits. They are instantly aware they are in spirit, but sometimes it takes a minute or so to shake off this life.

One misconception I have found is people believing that when someone passes, they walk through a tunnel of light to get to Heaven. There are people who have had what is known as a "near-death experience." These people passed away from an accident or on the operating table or any number of ways and were miraculously brought back to life. They claim that during this time, they experienced themselves leaving their bodies and going through a tunnel of light where they were greeted by family and friends in spirit. Even though that sounds like it might be quite an experience, I have found this not to be the case for most spirits.

In my experience with the spirits I have spoken with, this was not the case ... not for them anyway. I have even had spirits jokingly tell me and their loved ones receiving a reading that they were upset that they did not get to walk through the tunnel of light they'd heard so much about and thought maybe they were heading in the wrong direction! (Spirits always get a good laugh with that one.)

Do not get me wrong, I am not saying that these people who had a near-death experience did not see or experience what they are claiming they did, I believe in most cases they did. But perhaps this experience of the tunnel of light is only for those who are in fact going to be returning to this physical life and it is what is bringing them back into their bodies.

You may have also heard that when a person passes into spirit, they see their life flash before their eyes. This is true, but there is much more than just that, as not only do you see your whole life flash before your eyes, more importantly you feel the cause and effect of your entire life as well. It is the sum of how you spent your life here on Earth and it is what makes you who you are in spirit. This awakening takes place in a split second the moment you cross over.

And what one witnesses visually in spirit is quite amazing, breathtaking, and indescribable. First, a person KNOWS without a doubt that they are in spirit, in Heaven, and that life does continue. For most, it is a wonderful and joyous confirmation of what they had always believed or hoped, and to nonbelievers ... it is a happy surprise, to say the least.

As I mentioned before, Heaven is not a place that is separated from this physical world by location, but only by dimension. So when a person transitions into spirit, this new dimension becomes apparent along with the spirit continuing to be able to experience this one with their loved ones as well. It is like when you are in a dark room and you turn on the light—even though you are in the same room, once the light is on, everything around you becomes apparent. In spirit, this would be the light of God. And what becomes apparent is all that is Heaven ... and to say it is awe inspiring does not even come close.

As soon as the soul leaves the body and the awakening has occurred, the spirit will then be greeted by their loved ones who have passed before to welcome them home.

During this time in the passing, a spirit will also continue to experience what is taking place around them and at the same time participating in this physical world— from comforting those present during their passing, to going out and being beside someone who is receiving the news of their passing. This is why many times you have heard stories (and may have experienced it yourself) that someone gets a feeling, premonition, or whatever you want to call it, that a person has passed before they were ever told about it. This spirit is actually connecting with that person and is loving and consoling them.

A spirit will also witness and take part in everything that has to do with their passing, not only to help comfort their loved ones, but also to understand and comprehend how they have affected those they have touched in life.

And then after all of this is completed and life continues to move forward for everyone, the spirit enters the next chapter of their life and shares in all that Heaven and God are.

But most importantly, they will *continue* to love and participate in their loved ones' lives here on Earth as it is just as important to them as *anything* Heaven has to offer.

This is worth repeating ... *your loved ones in spirit remain with you and are a part of your life always.*

15: We Never Die Alone

One of the biggest regrets people sometimes have is when a loved one of theirs passes away alone.

It is natural for someone to want to be there when a loved one is going through the transition into spirit. They want to make sure that person is comfortable, know that their every need is being taking care of, and most of all, that they are not alone.

But sometimes due to the timing or countless other reasons, a person just cannot be there when a loved one has passed and that can cause a great deal of guilt or anguish.

Well, the truth of the matter is… no one ever passes alone.

When a person passes into spirit, the transition is as natural as the birth of a child. If you think about it, it is essentially the same thing as it is going from one realm into the next.

When the transition into spirit is taking place, much like in this physical realm when family members and friends take part in a birth … loved ones and friends in spirit are participating in the passing, making the dying person not alone at all!

———

Kathy and I had/have an aunt named Velma we would visit weekly. Velma lived in the home where my mother, Florence, and her eleven other brothers and sisters were born and raised. It was always comforting for us to be able to go to the place where so many generations had lived and also died. There was always such wonderful energy in that home.

As Velma started advancing in age, Kathy (who loves to cook) would make her homemade soups, smothered pork chops, or other favorites of Velma's to make sure she was eating right and keeping up her weight. Velma's favorite was always the homemade tapioca pudding as it reminded her of what her mother used to make for the family.

Eventually, Velma became ill and needed to be hospitalized. We would go and pay our aunt visits there, and each time she would be happy to see us. But as time went on, her illness became worse and took a toll on her appetite and with this came dramatic weight loss. We knew that she was not going to be getting better and that her time to cross over was inevitable.

One day when we went to visit Velma, as she lay in bed, Kathy asked if there was anything we could bring or do for her. She weakly replied no and said that she was just fine. She was hardly eating anything at this point as her appetite had all but vanished. So Kathy got an idea and told Velma that she would make her some tapioca pudding and bring it to her the next day. This caused a smile to appear on Velma's face and she told Kathy that the pudding would taste good. So the next day that is exactly what Kathy did and we brought over some tapioca pudding to her. At this point, our aunt was too weak to even feed herself so Kathy fed Velma her favorite dessert. While doing this Kathy told her she was going to fatten her up and again Velma got the biggest grin on her face.

After finishing the pudding, our aunt became more talkative but was still in a hazy state. As we were speaking with her, she perked up and all of a sudden told us that we needed to come to the cookout! Kathy and I looked at each other and instantly I started sensing loved ones in spirit surrounding all of us in the room. It was then we both knew exactly what was taking place; our loved ones in spirit were preparing Velma for her transition into life on the other side.

We continued speaking with her and asked her about the cookout and who all was there. She started naming all of her brothers, sisters, and other family members and friends who had passed long ago. She told us who was doing the cooking and described in detail all the delicious foods they were preparing. She was full of energy and emotion while she was describing the scene as if she was seeing it take place right before her eyes, which in fact she actually was! After filling us in on all the details, she began to tire and slowly fell asleep. Kathy and I knew that our family in spirit was preparing a big celebration for her and though we had to leave, we knew she was not alone.

Our aunt passed into spirit early the next morning.

———

Remember that it is always a gift to be able to converse with a loved one who is making the transition to the other side. Do not be surprised if you hear them speak about passed loved ones as if they are still alive as it is those loved ones who are helping them to cross over.

And remember that no one ever dies alone.

16: Reincarnation

The definition of reincarnation is the belief that the soul, upon the death of the body, eventually comes back to Earth in another body. Certainly, this can happen and really, why would that be so hard to believe?

You accept the fact that you have a soul and that your soul was born into your physical body. You believe that you will live your life and when you pass your soul leaves your body and goes to Heaven. If all of this is in fact true, why would it be so hard to accept that your soul cannot repeat this process more than once?

If this is really the case, why would people need to reincarnate in the first place?

When you went to school, you started in the first grade and once you completed learning your lessons in that grade, you went on to the next one and so on and so on. With every grade you attended, you were learning more until one day you completed all of your education and you graduated from school.

Well, this world is actually a big classroom for your soul and you are here to learn lessons in this lifetime. This can be done in one lifetime or it can take many, as it is up to the individual soul what they learn.

And if you ever have heard of someone having an "old soul," what this actually refers to is someone whose soul has aged with wisdom. This may even be you! Usually a person who is an old soul is someone who has always "felt" older than they were and seems to be wiser than most. Old souls usually worry a lot and even usually do not sleep well. Is this sounding familiar? And even though we are all here on this Earth to learn, old souls are also here as teachers, helping those around them learn in many diverse ways ... but more about old souls later.

Now you may be wondering if an animal can come back as a human or a human as an animal. In my opinion, I do not believe so, or let me just say that I have never spoken with anyone in spirit who has. But again, I have not spoken with everyone in spirit.

One time I was giving a reading at a demonstration to a woman when she stated that she was very close to her father. She told me that after he passed over, a gnat would follow her around every time she went outside and she was wondering if that could be her father. I asked her why in the world her father would want to come back in this world as a gnat. What would happen if she swatted him?

I told her that her father may be giving her a sign by having gnats fly around her if that represented the connection they had between them. But I assured her that her father did not come back as a bug.

———

There are various types of souls in this world, including humans, animals, and mammals. On the other side, there are these as well as other souls and beings such as angels. But no matter the differences of our souls, we all have one thing in common; we are all connected with God.

So does a soul ever stop being reincarnated?

Yes, but that is up to the soul. Your soul can stop coming back when you have grown as much or taught as much as you should. Again, this can happen in one lifetime or it can take many; it is up to you how much and how fast you learn during your time here on Earth.

But before you start to worry that you might miss a loved one who passes before you get over there...do not worry! Reincarnation usually takes many decades if not centuries for a soul to return here, if at all. So rest assured you'll see grandma or any of your other loved ones in spirit again before, or if, either they or you decide to come back.

17: GHOSTS & HAUNTINGS

Remember when you were a child and you and your friends would get together on a stormy night with the wind howling through the trees outside and lightning and the sound of thunder rolling closer and closer by the minute? You would huddle in the darkest corner of the house with a flashlight and try to scare each other by telling ghost stories. I sure do.

But in reality are there actually such things as ghosts?

When people hear the word "ghost," many call up the image of a lost or trapped soul of a person who is either visiting or stuck here in this physical plane for years and years. Perhaps they arrive at this interpretation of a ghost by remembering a story they may have read or been told as kids, books they have read, or television shows and films they may have seen. These sources, as well as others relating to ghosts, will usually give the impression or insinuate that a ghost is usually connected with negativity or evil.

The fact of the matter is that there *are* such things as ghosts, just not as described above.

In the real world, a "ghost" is just another name for a "spirit," with no difference at all between the two. (But for this section of the book, I will continue to use the term "ghost" because we are talking about the "paranormal" and it just sounds scarier.) When someone comes in contact with a ghost, for the most part it is usually just a person's loved one in spirit!

Now when a person experiences a ghost, this connection could be as little as seeing movement out of the corner of the eye to actually seeing part or a whole figure of a person standing or walking in a house or even outdoors. A ghost can appear in visible form or other manifestations, from an invisible presence to translucent or wispy shapes, to realistic, life-like figures. What can make an encounter with a ghost seem more frightening is that the experience will usually happen when a person is not expecting it, and thereby they become significantly startled by the unforeseen visit. Let's just say that you will usually not hear a ghost walking up to you.

As mentioned in my previous book, *Never Say Goodbye*, the first time I recall seeing a ghost was at the age of six, that being the ghost of my uncle who had passed a few weeks prior. I won't go into detail as I have in that book, but suffice it to say he simply wanted to communicate with me to let the family know he was doing just fine! He wasn't haunting me or trying to scare me, not at all. He just wanted to relay the message.

Additional reasons why ghosts have a negative perception connected with them is due to some people's religious beliefs, thereby making ghosts themselves or even connecting with them something unnatural, maybe even evil.

———

I remember once while doing a book signing, a gentleman asked me to sign my book for him and then asked what my thoughts were on "shadow people." Some people believe that shadow people are dark figures or entities that are supposedly malicious or evil spirits that one may see out of their peripheral vision (or out of the corner of their eye).

This man nervously told me that he saw shadow people from time to time and he was taught that they were evil entities. He said that he had been praying to his loved ones in spirit to help him but apparently they would not because he continued to see the shadow people.

I could not help but smile and informed this man that it was probably his loved ones in spirit whom he had been praying to that were the "shadow people" he was seeing! Taken back by this, he said that he was not sure if he believed me. So I asked him if any of these so-called shadow people had ever done anything that would give him the impression that they were evil or harmful. He thought hard about it and replied that they had not. At the same time this conversation was taking place, I could not help but notice there was a mother in spirit standing in front of me trying to get my attention. It was not hard for me to put two and two together, so I asked this man if his mother had passed. Surprised by my question, he replied that she had. So I quickly turned my attention to her and asked if she had a quick message for her son. She said that it was in fact herself as well as his father in spirit that he kept seeing, because they were still looking after him, and he should not to be afraid of the "ghosts"! "After all, your mother is telling me that you took great care of her when she was sick and that it meant so much for you to be there for her." She wanted me to tell him that now she was there for her baby!

After delivering this message, I could tell it brought relief to the man's mind and he thanked me for helping him.

And that really is the key to not being afraid of ghosts and to "understanding" what they are.

Let's break down a few more myths about ghosts...

One myth is that when a ghost first enters a room, a person will feel a cold temperature and maybe even experience goose bumps (the scientific term for these are *cutis anserine*) on their arms. Yes, that can happen to a person sensing a spirit. The reason why people are experiencing this is because their body is reacting to the energy of what is taking place.

When someone becomes scared or frightened, the sensitivity of the nerves in the body is heightened, thereby making the individual feel that the temperature around them is changing, when in fact it is not. It is a natural body reaction to sensing a spirit, which can come in the form of a hot or cold temperature change.

Another myth similar to the example above about "shadow people" is that people think when they capture an image of a dark shape or a dark mass on film that it is a negative or evil spirit because of the dark color. This also is not true. The color of a spirit seen by the eye or captured on film has absolutely nothing to do with its being good or bad; it is only the way your eyes or the film have seen or captured it.

Kathy and I conducted a haunting investigation at the Poe Museum in Richmond, Virginia, with a small group of eager novice ghost hunters. The Poe Museum is a fantastic place to visit with its rich history, and a wonderful place to investigate. We had just taken a break when one of the participants came rushing over to Kathy and I, excited by what she had caught on her camera. "Look, look!" she exclaimed. "I have captured some dark evil presence hovering in the garden." As we both viewed the screen of her camera, we did see a small dark fuzzy shape in the corner of the garden. But after careful examination of her camera and also the side of her chin, we knew it was not a ghost's image she had caught. It was instead a smudge of peanut butter on her camera lens from a sandwich she had just eaten. Kathy and I applauded the effort and enthusiasm though.

Another myth is that when a person sees a spirit out of the corner of their eye, the ghost disappears the moment they turn to look at it. Truth be told, the spirit actually does not leave and in fact is still standing there. The reason they seem to disappear is because when a person sees a spirit out of the corner of their eye, they are using their peripheral vision, which can be connected with a person's sixth sense. But out of habit, a person will automatically turn to see what is standing beside them, breaking their connection with the sight of the spirit. If this happens to you, the best thing to do is to not turn your head. I know it is difficult, but by not turning your head, you will see the spirit standing there even longer!

So yes, ghosts really do exist, but if you ever see one, it is probably just a loved one in spirit paying a visit!

———

Now when people think of a haunted house, eerie images of ghosts and lost souls wandering through a house may come to mind. The perception is that these spirits are wreaking havoc in the house because they are trapped in it due to a negative experience they had there or because they want the people who are occupying the house to leave!

But can a house truly be haunted?

The answer to that question is yes and no. Hold on, and before you start becoming terrified, read on…

To begin with, if having a ghost or a spirit in a house makes it haunted, then guess what, every house in the world is in fact haunted!

Every person on this Earth has loved ones in spirit who visit them in their home on a daily basis. At times, spirits will make their presence known by giving a physical sign or a person will even sense them in a house. The only problem when this occurs is that most of the time a person is unaware of who or what is giving the sign and they leap to the conclusion that their house is haunted. Funny how many people will ask for signs from a loved one in spirit and as soon as they receive one, they become frightened.

Once at a demonstration Kathy and I were giving, a woman almost jumped out of her seat when our question-and-answer session of the night started. Kathy went to her right away with the microphone in hand and asked this woman what her question or comment was. The woman stood up, shaking, and told me that she knew for a fact that her house was haunted and she and her family were completely terrified. Several gasps could be heard throughout the room. When I asked her why she thought this, she said she had experienced many scary occurrences taking place such as pictures moving on the wall by themselves, noises coming out of nowhere, as well as even feeling the entities around her during the dark of the night, especially when she was alone in the house and very scared. Knowing what was probably going on, I asked if she had been asking for signs from her loved ones in spirit. She looked at me as if I was trying to change the subject and she replied that she had, but what did that have to do with anything. I asked her what specific signs she had requested that her loved ones in spirit give her, and she replied that she did not request anything specific. So my final question to her was if she had not asked for something specific, how was she going to know when a sign appeared? Sheepishly she lowered her head and told me she just thought she would know. So I assured this woman that she had in fact been receiving signs from her family members who had passed, and had been mistaking them for her house being haunted. I reminded her that she said she even "felt" them when she was at her most vulnerable, when she was alone and scared. That is the time when your loved ones step it up and try to comfort you the most. She smacked her own forehead with her hand as if a light had come on and she laughed. She realized that it all fit now and made perfect sense. She promised she would recognize the indications of her loved ones' presence and try not to be frightened by them again.

So when you do hear noises coming from a wall or lights blinking in your home, it is not that your house is haunted, but loved ones in spirit are letting you know they are there with you … most of the time.

Now you may be wondering if a house can have a ghost in it that is not a loved one in spirit.

The answer is yes, it can.

If someone lives in an old house, usually there will be a lot of history connected with that house such as past families who have lived there. Even though a house is just a house, the important part of it is what a person's feelings and experiences in that house have been that make it a home. Spirits do like to revisit such locations to check up on what is taking place there, just as you may have done with an old house you used to live in. But these visitors only come for a short visit and in fact are usually accompanied by your loved ones who have passed.

Keep in mind it is not only houses that spirits will visit, but any buildings or land with which a spirit once had a connection.

Kathy and I have been lucky enough to have travelled to many places around the world investigating locations where paranormal activity has been documented. Anytime we visit a supposed haunted location, we go with the knowledge that if we are going to encounter a ghost there, it is not necessarily because of negative reasons such as the ghost being trapped there. We know they are visiting as well, and may want to share information about themselves or the history of or their experiences in this place.

Remember, ghosts are people too, and sometimes they have something they would like to have known, or at times, even have some fun…

———

We were in Manchester, England, to film episodes of the television show *Most Haunted*. Once we arrived and our plane landed, we were picked up by a car at the airport and driven straight to our hotel. It was a beautiful morning and after flying all night, it was very refreshing to breathe in some good clean air and take in some of the sights as we made our way to the hotel. As we approached the hotel, it was easy to see from the exterior that it was an extremely old building, one that probably had much history associated with it, but once we entered, it was a totally different story as the interior of the building had been completely remodeled with a very modern chic red-and-black décor, a nice look if you are into that type of style.

Once we checked in and were settled in our room, relaxing after our long journey, Kathy and I began to discuss the filming schedule for the show, wondering which haunted locations we would be visiting. With

Most Haunted, we were never told the location where the investigation was going to take place, in order to keep the integrity of what I did intact. This was not only a rule of the show, but also important to me.

The subject then turned to our hotel room. We thought the building was not originally a hotel as it seemed a bit industrial. Another old warehouse-like building was behind us. It was being renovated at the moment and the top floor was old and creepy. Dark and mysterious with several window panes broken out, the sun barely lit the abandoned floor as thoughts of the past filled our heads. We started brainstorming about what our hotel might have been in the past. Even though often when we do investigations we both can actually pick up on past events that have taken place at a location, we were both dead tired (excuse the pun), and did not feel like opening our senses up to see if we could perceive anything... or anyone. But at that moment while we were having this discussion, we both heard a loud noise coming from the bathroom. We knew we were the only ones in the room, so we jumped up to see if anyone else had entered. As we slowly opened the door and started to search the bathroom, we noticed that the metal stopper for the sink had somehow jumped out and landed on the floor. We looked at each other and smiled because not only had we just used the bathroom and saw the stopper was in the sink, but we knew at that moment a ghost in the room was making its presence known to us.

Kathy thanked the hotel ghost out loud for the sign and as we left the bathroom and headed back to our beds again, we realized that the ghosts were not quite through with us yet. We had received another sign from them—the television remote control was lying on top of one of the beds with all of its batteries scattered out of the device. Again, we knew neither one of us had even held the remote, so we thanked the ghost or ghosts again and knew we were going to be in for a good time during this visit.

We were not disappointed…

———

In this example of a haunting, the experience we had just encountered could have been taken in one of two ways. The first is that our rooms were haunted by evil ghosts and we were disturbing them with our presence there. The second (which is more likely) is that the spirits were listening to our conversation and wanted to have some fun with us.

So when it comes to ghosts and hauntings, again there really is nothing, for the most part, to be afraid of as it is usually the spirit of a loved one making their presence known.

———

Now you may be wondering, can a person, now in spirit, who was negative or bad, cause harm to anyone here?

Yes and no, depending on the situation.

First, if the negativity in a person was caused by a mental disorder or even substance abuse (as it is with most cases), this person in spirit will no longer have this condition and they will be transformed into a positive spirit.

Remember that once in spirit your mind is clear and the reasons for abuse are understood.

If a person was just a negative human being because of their personality, once they pass into spirit, they can have a much greater understanding of the cause and effects of their actions and will usually take the required steps to learn from their actions.

But on rare occasions, spirits sometimes will react to someone who is provoking or asking them to do something physically to them. This would be the same as, let's say, during the day you were out taking a walk and you passed people along the way. You may smile at them and even say hello, but there probably would not be any physical contact with them. But say you took that same walk and as you were walking, you were asking everyone whom you passed to push you or even hurt you in a physical way. Though most people you pass would probably just look at you as if you were crazy, you would probably run across a few who would be more than happy to give you what you asked for. This is the same way with ghosts—if a person is asking for a spirit to do something to them physically or if the person is provoking the spirit, thereby making them angry, they may very well get what they ask for.

When I am on paranormal investigations, even though I can make a connection with a spirit and speak with them, I also will open myself up for any form of contact they want to have, including doing something to me physically.

I remember a few Halloweens ago; I was in Gettysburg, Pennsylvania, on a paranormal investigation that was being broadcast on live television around the United States. I had never been to Gettysburg before and found it to be quite a charming and, yes, haunted town. The quaint streets with the beautiful old homes were lined with pumpkins and cornstalks. There was a palpable energy in the air.

During the night, as a cold October chill set in, the investigation team and I were walking around the attic of a historical old home. I felt the strong presence of a spirit who wanted to communicate with me. As I started to relay messages, the other investigators started provoking the spirit I was in contact with. All of a sudden, I felt this spirit starting to drain all of my energy from me and the next thing I knew, I had fallen to the ground on my knees! Again, I guess I should have watched what I asked for! It only took me a minute or so to gain my energy back, but as we went on with the investigation something else would soon happen to me again physically.

The investigations were going great as we went to several historic homes that night with fantastic results. With dawn only a few hours away, I made a connection with a Civil War soldier who wanted very much to communicate. Usually when I connect with a spirit, they will convey to me how they passed over by letting me have a slight sensation of what they felt at the time of their passing. When this occurs, this sensation usually only lasts a few seconds and then the feeling disappears. But since I was extra sensitive during the investigation, when this soldier gave me the feeling that he died from being stabbed in the back, the feeling he gave was extremely tense and it actually was very physically painful for me to experience. In fact, I had a backache for the entire week afterward.

But again, I asked for this to happen.

For the most part, all ghosts, loved ones or not, will do what you ask them to do, so if you are in fact uncomfortable with noticing them in your home, tell them not to come or at least not to let their presence be known. Many times a spirit will have to be with you in order to help you with an event or problem in your life. That is part of what your loved ones do in spirit. But if you are not comfortable with them making their presence known, just say so.

I also get asked quite often if spirits are "always" around and my answer is, never worry about your "private time" in your home, a ghost knows when to leave a room …

What is referred to as a residual haunting is very different than a haunting by a spirit, as it is not actually even a haunting at all.

This phenomenon takes place when the energy of an event that has taken place in the past is either sensed by an individual seeing it, hearing it, or it is being picked up on film.

Everything we do in this life leaves an impression (think of it as a thumbprint of energy) in the physical world. It is as if this planet is one big recorder and our lives and our actions are being recorded. The stronger the event or occurrence that takes place in our lives, the more energy or the greater the thumbprint it will leave behind.

Usually older homes or locations can have residual hauntings since they have had more life experiences taking place there, and with that comes more energy that has been left behind. Also places where tragedies have occurred, such as battlefields, have been known to produce very intense experiences in residual hauntings. Many people have reported seeing, hearing, or sensing some portion of a past battle being played out, mistaking this to be taking place in real time. In reality what they are picking up on is something that has taken place in the past. If this phenomenon occurs at a regular time or date and is the same action over and over again, it is likely a residual haunting.

Anytime I do an investigation of a historic location, I will open myself up to the "history" of it to see if I can pick up on any past events that have taken place there. By doing so, when I am able to discern something, what I experience is like seeing an overlay of the past laid on top of the present. Think of it this way; it is as if you were to take a movie of a location today and then place a transparent movie of the same location from the past over it. I see both today and yesterday taking place simultaneously.

———

I remember in one of the *Most Haunted* episodes, I, along with Karl, Yvette, and the rest of the team, were on a very old and historical pier in southeast England to see what I was able to pick up. It was quite a chilly day and the wind was whipping across the sea. As I opened up my senses and looked out onto the shoreline, I started to see a visual in front of me coming into focus. I physically saw where the coastline was at that moment, but I also saw where in the past it extended out even farther. I saw that at one time there had been land where the ocean was now, with what I

took to be a castle standing tall, and many people perform-
ing their daily tasks.

Of course, as I was explaining this to the team, I had
no idea what I was seeing, but fortunately the historian,
Lesley (or Lady Lesley, as Kathy likes to refer to her), who
was part of the team did. She explained that in the specific area I was pointing to, in the past, there was in fact
land that people did inhabit, as well as a church (which
would have had turrets and certainly looked like a castle,
she confirmed) once standing on that very spot. But as the
centuries passed, the sea eventually took over that area of
the country, burying that town along with its history.

———

Even though I am able to do this at will, some people and
even devices such as cameras and audio/video recorders
can also detect these events sporadically at times. You,
yourself, may have even experienced this to a smaller
degree and not realized it. Have you ever walked into a
room or building where you could sense a negative event
that has taken place there and could feel the bad energy
still lurking in the present? That is because you picked
up on that energy or the residual haunting of the event
that occurred. So do open yourself up when visiting such
places in the future as you never know what past events
you may experience for yourself!

18: Lost or Trapped Souls

Some believe that if a person experiences an unexpected passing due to a tragic trauma such as an accident, murder, or suicide, that person's soul can become trapped or lost. They think of these spirits as being stuck in-between this world and the next, roaming aimlessly for decades or even centuries, maybe even totally unaware that their life has ended.

You may even have seen so-called mediums or psychics on television shows that will go to a location that supposedly has a trapped or lost soul in it and start shouting to that spirit that they are in fact dead and need to move on and walk into the light.

I remember watching one television show that featured several so-called mediums holding a séance to see what spirits would come through and give messages from beyond.

Taking place in an old theater, the scene was set up in a dark room with the participants seated in a circle holding hands. Lit only by candles, the medium at the head of the table began to tremble and moan. Although their original intent was to try to reach a certain man associated with the theater, the lost soul of a woman began to come through. The medium made a "connection" with a mother in spirit who had supposedly been lost, trapped for decades in this building in search of her little boy, also in spirit. The medium began channeling the woman, relaying through tears streaming down her face that she had been searching for her son in spirit and stating how much pain and torment she was in not having found him. When the other mediums who were participants in this séance informed this spirit that she was in fact dead, the spirit of the woman could not believe it!

So luckily, by chance (and I mean that sarcastically), one of the other mediums happened to connect with this woman's son who too had been searching for his mother for decades. Now, let's get this straight. Not only had the poor mother been "lost" for decades, but she, and her son as well, had been searching aimlessly in this old abandoned theater for each other, and I guess just never ran into each other. But because of these wonderful mediums and the séance, the two spirits finally became reunited and they were then instructed by the other participants of the séance to go into the light, which they then supposedly proceeded to do—another happy ending … The End.

All I can say is thank God for this female spirit that these mediums decided to hold a séance and told her to go into the light, or the spirits of this mother and child may have been roaming around for all eternity! (Again, I am being sarcastic.) What did these spirits say to themselves: "Oh, we are dead? We were wondering why no one had been talking with us for all of this time. And the light we never thought about walking into it. Gee, we are so glad this living person came along and told us that we are dead and how to go to Heaven."

Really … really?

It is as if these souls have been wandering aimlessly for years and years, not realizing they are dead and it took some stranger to yell it out to them before they finally realized the truth.

Do they think that spirits who pass in a tragic way lose their common sense or something?

So no, there is no such thing as a lost or trapped soul.

If you really think about it, would the soul of such a person not have their loved ones and friends in spirit come and help them? Oh yeah … and then there is God! Did he just forget about these spirits and leave them walking this Earth for all eternity, waiting for a medium to come and tell them to simply walk into the light? To believe something like this is attributing a lot of ignorance to spirits as well as Heaven and God. Shouting out a command assumes we possess power over a spirit that we really do not have.

You may be wondering: why would a "ghost" or spirit just be hanging out at a location for years or even centuries?

Well, they really do not do that either.

Just as I discussed with "hauntings," saying that a spirit is able to view and interact in this physical realm, they also like to visit locations from their past to check out how these places may have changed or what is taking place there now. But these souls are just visiting and are not stuck for any period of time. They also may have a story to tell and their presence may shed light on that history.

Anytime I perform paranormal investigations of a historical location, I know the spirits I come in contact with are not imprisoned there. More times than not, these are just souls who want to make a connection with me in order to share in the experience of communicating with a medium as well as wanting to reveal some events and history that have taken place at the location.

———

I once investigated what was known to be some very haunted woods in England. It is one thing to go to a centuries-old castle or an old structure that has had people from the past tied to it, but woods? I knew this was going to be a challenge!

The area of the haunted woods was vast and hilly. I was immediately drawn to an overgrown spot on top of a hill. As I was walking through a small clearing in the thick, wooded area, I actually started to pick up on several people in spirit who were also in the woods. I decided to move slowly down the ravine and as I did, one of the spirits began to make his connection with me even stronger. It was the spirit of a young soldier. This young warrior told me that he had been a Roman soldier many centuries ago and shared with me an interesting account about his life. I could feel how brave this man was in this life and his soul was filled with honor.

Now, had this soldier been walking around in the woods forever waiting to speak with me? No. This spirit had a history in these woods and once I called out for someone who had a connection with the place, he came to tell his story … leaving right afterward.

———

So, in my experience, the spirits I have come across have never been trapped or lost between this physical world and the other side … as there is no in between.

19: Animal Heaven

One of the most frequently asked questions I receive is from people who want to know, do their pets go to Heaven? And the answer is … of course they do!

Some people think there is another Heaven for animals, but this is not the case at all. We all go to the same place when we pass over and that includes our beloved pets!

I am often asked if I am able to communicate with a person's pet that has passed. I am in fact able to do this, but not quite in the same way as I connect with humans. I will tell people that the spirit of a pet will not come up to me and start speaking English as their human loved ones in spirit will do, but their pets are able to communicate with me through their thoughts and feelings. A pet can show me images of events in my mind as well as communicate the emotions they feel for their owners.

A client named Olivia had come to me several times in the past in order for me to connect with her family and friends in spirit. On one occasion, Olivia was finding it hard to make a decision and came to me for guidance. Her beloved cat that she'd had for many years had recently passed and she was feeling guilty about adopting another.

"I have your mother here and she is in fact holding your cat," I told Olivia.

Olivia began to tear up, saying, "My baby! I was hoping she would have her there."

"She says she does and she also wants you to know that it was the right decision," I replied.

With that, Olivia really began to weep.

"Her kidneys were failing and even though the doctor told me I had little choice but to put her down, I did not know if I should," Olivia responded, her voice quivering.

"Your cat is giving me not only the feeling of the immense love she has for you but also a positive feeling that it was in fact the right thing to do. It was just her time to be in spirit," I affirmed.

Olivia closed her eyes slowly, tears streaming down her cheeks but with a look of relief on her face.

I continued, "Your cat also is showing me another cat with you, do you have another?"

"No, and that is what I wanted to know! I loved Ms. Kitty so much that I do not want her to think that I don't love her anymore if I adopt another."

"This is why she is showing me another cat with you. Not only is she not upset, she is actually going to help you find the next one!" I said.

Olivia asked, "She is?"

"Yes, as you look for the right cat, she is going to give you a 'gut instinct' so you will know which one is the right one to get."

"I didn't know she could do that," Olivia said.

I replied, "Sure she can, she has a great energy around her so I would not be surprised if you feel her around you."

Excitedly, Olivia responded, "I do! I do think I feel her around me! I just thought that it was my imagination."

"Now you know it's not. Just like when experiencing the presence of your mother and father, or any of your loved ones in spirit with you, the same can happen with your pets," I said.

She replied, "Well, I can't tell you how happy that makes me, knowing that Ms. Kitty is safe and still loves me and will help me with this."

"Also make sure that, once you get a new cat, you watch him or her for any signs of Ms. Kitty messing around. Pets in spirit are known to do such things, you know!"

"I will!" said Olivia.

A month or so later, Olivia e-mailed me a picture of herself holding her brand new kitten, one that she felt Ms. Kitty helped her pick out. She decided to rightly name her new kitten "Mr. Kitty."

———

If you have a pet that has passed away, make sure you keep talking to them and loving them—they are still running around your house or land and still love you very much. And do not forget that they too can give you signs of their presence, so keep an eye out!

PART 3
THIS LIFE

As spirit first, our goal in living this physical life is to ascend into becoming our highest self, which in turn brings us closer to God. In order for this to be accomplished, our souls need to experience different situations that can only exist in this physical world, as many opportunities for soul growth can come from the negative experiences that we encounter, something that does not exist in Heaven.

This section explains why we are living this physical life, what lessons can be learned while we are here, and what can be done to live a more fulfilling one.

20: Classroom Called Life

Since we are spirit first, and our soul has come from Heaven, you may be wondering why it is that you are living in this physical world.

The short answer is that you are living this life in order to experience certain situations and challenges (those that occur naturally as well as those that are self-caused) that can only take place in this physical world in order for you to learn, which in turn gives your soul the opportunity for growth.

If you were to reminisce back to the time when you went to school, you probably would remember that there were good times and bad times, as well as everything in between, during that period in your life. Each grade you attended taught you many lessons, not only through the various tests you took, but also through the way you associated with other classmates, the way you dealt with your teachers, and countless other circumstances you encountered. After you completed all the lessons that you needed to learn in one grade, you advanced on to the next one in order to continue to heighten your education.

So, think of this world as one enormous classroom, but here the lessons are not for your mind, but for your soul.

When you are born into this life, you come here with what you can refer to as an outline or a lesson plan with certain events and situations that can and will take place in your life. But as in school, your soul also possesses freedom of choice, if you are of sound mind, as to how you will act or react to any situation you might encounter. Every decision you make, every deed you do, and every thought you have determine your soul's growth in this life.

Life lessons can come in any number of ways, shapes, and forms, and they are endless. To list each of them or to even categorize them all would be an impossible task, but let's touch on a few.

HEALTH LESSONS

One of the strongest and most intense situations that can generate the most emotion from a person is when they are experiencing or know someone who is dealing with a health issue.

Being healthy is the most important aspect of anyone's life, yet it is also the one most people take for granted. Once you or someone you know loses their health, not only can it be life-changing, but soul-changing as well.

The truth is that God has not designed the "health" of the physical body to last forever, as it is only your soul that is eternal. There is a time to live on this Earth, and at some point there is going to be a time to return to spirit. When that time does come, it will be due to some negative health issue that has happened in the physical body. Even though it can seem that, for some people, going through specific health issues might be harsh, unjustified, and even cruel at times (especially if it is a child experiencing this), there is always a reason for it to take place, and that reason is for soul growth and its fulfillment, not only for the person who has the health issue, but even more so for those who are connected with them.

I recall giving a reading once to a man named George who was diagnosed with a sudden illness and given only a few months to live. A situation like this can be one of the most challenging (and at the same time rewarding) for someone, along with their family.

By the time I spoke with George, he was already bed-ridden and required twenty-four-hour care. Although his voice was weak, he was still able to communicate very well over the phone with me. I connected to his wife who was in spirit and through her messages was able to bring much comfort and peace to this man. George told his wife that he felt very remorseful that their four children had to take care of him now as he did not want to be a burden on them. His wife told him that not only was he not a burden, but he was actually giving them a gift, one that they could all cherish. Asking what in the world she was speaking about, George's wife explained that the gift was the opportunity for his family to do the most important thing that any person can do in this life and that is for his family to be able to help him, take care of him, and most of all to love him. She said she could "feel" how much it meant for them to be able to take care of their father, and reminded George that it was the same way he had taken care of her eight years before.

I did hear back from George's family. They wanted me to know how much their mother's messages had helped their father during his last days, and how he did, in fact, give in to letting them do what they wanted to do most of all, and that was to take care of him and to love him.

This loving message from his wife very much eased his guilt as he knew that he did take care of his wife and considered the time he had spent with her during her illness very precious. Ever since her passing, he would reflect back on how much it meant to him to have been by her side, taking care of her. It was a present from her to him and now he was passing the same gift on to his children.

One of the greatest offerings God has given to people in this life is the ability to help someone who is sick or dying. It can be someone who may just have sprained an ankle and needs help getting around or someone who is taking their last breath and needs a hand to hold. These lessons appear in so many ways.

I have come across many people in my life who have been provided with just such an opportunity of helping a loved one. Be it for a parent or grandparent, relative or friend, some of these people did not think twice about being there for that sick person and doing everything in their power to make sure they were as comfortable and well loved as possible.

But there are others I have come across who found the challenge of having to deal with someone who was sick to be a burden on their lives and they gave little service or even pulled away from the situation completely. These people are missing out on the opportunity of a lifetime. Be it through wanting forgiveness for a wrong done by either party or just a wish to strengthen the bond of love between them, these times provide amazing results where relationships can heal or the love that is shared becomes stronger.

One of the biggest regrets I hear from people is the "would of, should of, could of" when they were given the opportunity to help an unhealthy loved one.

NATURE'S LESSONS

There are also events people will encounter in this life that are another way God is giving us an opportunity for soul growth, and that is through "nature" or what is also referred to as "acts of God."

Throughout history, individuals have believed that when natural disasters occur such as floods, earthquakes, hurricanes, and tornados, they are God's way of showing his wrath.

In actuality, it is quite the opposite.

As mentioned before, God does not punish anyone on this Earth nor does he have a temper—as he is all-loving and never vengeful, as some choose to believe. But it is actually with these acts of nature that God gives people the chance to help, to love, and to heal those in need, which in turn gives the soul another opportunity for growth.

I remember experiencing the Northridge Earthquake in Los Angeles, California. This was one of the biggest quakes in recent times. While asleep one night, I had awakened abruptly as I was tossed violently out of my bed. At that moment, I realized what was taking place as there is no mistaking an earthquake, and my home was shaking so hard that all I could do was get on my hands and knees and hope for the best as I rode it out. I remember, as the house and everything in it was shaking and falling all around me, I was shouting out to Kathy to wake up, hoping she would be able to hear me from her room, not that she wasn't already awake … but it was still instinct to do this. The noise was quite memorable: it sounded like a freight train was coming through our house.

After what seemed forever, but in actual time was a minute or so, the earthquake was over. As I got up and ran out of my room, stepping over the objects that had fallen, I met up with Kathy down the hall and she too was shaken but all right. Stunned, we both pulled ourselves together and looked around our home. Even though much had fallen and crashed to the floor, it seemed that our home had not suffered major damage in the quake. So, as we were well and unharmed, we quickly went back to our rooms and threw on some clothes, then headed outside. The night was exceptionally dark as there was no electricity to light the streets. Everyone in the neighborhood was coming out of their homes and buzzed about what each had just experienced. People were asking each other if they were hurt, as well as what damage had taken place. Fortunately, besides a scrape, bump, or bruise that some received, everyone near us was fine and the quake did only minor damage to the surrounding structures. This was not just happening in my neighborhood, it was taking place all around the city. Even though there was only minor damage caused by the quake where I lived, there were many areas in and around Los Angeles that were destroyed, and people came from all over to offer help in any way they could to those who were in need. People who were strangers to each other were offering aid to the victims.

Thus, during these natural disasters, selfishness, prejudice, and apathy often fall by the wayside, replaced by the emotions of caring, selflessness, and love that can come to the forefront. These positive feelings and emotions are always a part of us; sometimes it takes an act of nature to remind us that they are within us.

HUMAN LESSONS

Another way people learn lessons in this life is through the conflicts they create. By this I mean challenges that are caused not by health issues or nature, but by people. Sometimes these conflicts can be more difficult to learn from, but also may prove to be more rewarding than with any other lessons.

These lessons begin with one thing and one thing only, and that is perception. By perception, I mean a person's point of view on anything related to living in this life. There are many ideas and beliefs that people share, but there are also many that people differ on, since perception is as unique as every individual.

In this world, everyone of a sound state of mind is born with the knowledge of what is right, what is wrong, what is good, or what is bad. This is the natural compass we all possess that helps to guide us to the paths and roads we want to take in our life. The basic needs we all share in this world are those of survival, love, and the pursuit of happiness ... they are the essence of our physical lives. It is these inherited instincts that place us all on common ground.

Along with the basic needs we share comes a second layer that makes us who we are, and that is comprised of our own perspectives and emotions. It is this layer that separates each of us as individuals.

An example of this would be the following:

Everyone in this world would agree that on a nice clear, sunny day, the color of the sky is blue. But due to perception, the shade of blue that someone can see in the sky could be slightly different than the shade of blue someone else sees. Again, it is the same shade we physically witness in the sky; the only difference is how we perceive it. And with your personal perceptions also comes the formation of your own opinions. For example, do you like the tint of blue in the sky? Obviously there is no right or wrong answer to this question as it is what your personal opinions and feelings are that matter.

Being an individual with your own unique likes and dislikes is what guides you in making choices in life. What you eat, what clothes you wear, what entertains you—all of these traits add up and help to define who you are. And with all of these factors, even though you may have a different perspective than others do, you can still respect another person's point of view, as their opinions have no direct effect on your own personal life.

But then there are the factors on which people can have different perspectives and points of view that can affect someone else's life.

For example, you would probably agree that it would be clearly wrong for someone to inflict pain on another for no reason. Also, by the same token, you would probably agree that it would be acceptable for you to hurt someone else if you were defending yourself.

Though most people do not condone causing physical harm for no reason, most would agree it is permissible in the case of self-defense.

But how about if you were to lash out physically just because someone said something that made you angry? For instance, let's say if someone approached you and started talking trash about one of your family members. Would it be okay to push or hit that person?

Now some of you may feel you should never physically harm someone just because of what they have said, while others of you may feel it certainly is acceptable to do so because the person was asking for it.

Is there a right answer or wrong answer to this question, or does it depend on what your own personal perception or opinion is of the situation?

Ah, you see, this is where many disagreements and conflicts begin in this life, by the differing perspectives people have.

But with this also comes the opportunity for more life lessons.

Many of the controversies people have faced in this life began when a person's belief or point of view did not coincide with someone else's and this is when physical or psychological action has taken place. From social issues, to ideological thought, to varying cultures, to trade, differences of opinions on all of these have created conflict in our world since the beginning of time. But again, it is with these quandaries that opportunities come into play, allowing people to develop and use personal feelings such as compassion, understanding, patience, and love—all of which take the soul to a higher level.

This growth of the soul can take place instantaneously once the opportunity presents itself, or it can take an entire lifetime of contemplation, or it may not even be learned at all.

It is always up to you.

EVERYDAY LESSONS

With the examples you have just read, you can see these lessons take place when a person is forced to react, be it to an illness, natural disaster, or conflict. But you may not ever go through a natural disaster yourself or experience a loved one becoming ill anytime soon. So how then are lessons learned when these situations are not taking place in your life?

Simple ... instead of waiting to react ... act!

All you need to do is look around in your neighborhood, at a newspaper, or even turn on the television to find a way to heighten your spirit. There are always people in this world in need of a helping hand. From donating money to helping feed starving children, or helping an elderly parent or neighbor living just down the street, countless opportunities are present each and every day. It only takes a moment to identify what they are, and sometimes all it takes is for you to share that moment in time with someone to make all the difference in the world.

No matter how small or how large, everything you do for someone else matters in this life for your soul's growth ... that is if it comes from the right place.

Though living this life and doing for others can help with your soul's growth, it is not necessarily the actual physical act of doing something that is increasing that growth, but the feelings that you have behind the act that are what count, as emotions are what build the foundation of your soul.

I once spoke with a man who told me very brashly that he was going straight to Heaven. When I asked him why he thought this, he told me that he had just given a charity a large sum of money and he knew it was "the right thing to do." I responded by saying that it was kind of him to give such a donation and helping people was always the right thing to do. He then started to laugh and said that even though it was great that he was helping people, what he meant by the "right thing to do" was that it was going to help him with his taxes.

This is an example of where something charitable was done, but for the wrong reason. Even though this man was in fact helping others, the deed was done only to benefit himself. And with that, the lesson was lost.

Always remember that God smiles at those who give aid to the many who seek it, but smiles broader at those who seek out the many who are in need.

———

In conclusion, when you are feeling happiness, patience, sympathy, or compassion, all of these are positive feelings that enlighten the being of who you are. But your soul can also experience negative feelings such as anger, hate, resentment, and jealousy, thereby lowering the soul's energy level.

Now before you start worrying because you have experienced negative emotions, do not. Everyone has experienced all of these emotions some time or another. What is important is to increase the positive emotions that you have and decrease and diminish the negative ones. This can be as easy or as hard as you make it—it is up to you.

Think about it. Every thought that you have ever had and every action that you have taken is what has made you who you are today. And the more enlightened and enriched your soul becomes in this life through every lesson you encounter, the higher your spirit level will be...which in turn brings you closer to God.

The most important lesson that people are here to learn in this life is that of love, as love is truly the essence of all of that God is.

21: OLD SOULS

You have heard the term, old soul, but you may be wondering what it means.

Old souls are people whose spirits have lived on this Earth numerous times before through reincarnation. By having done so, their soul has increased knowledge through every life experience and they have a deep understanding of how to live as well as possess a well-balanced character. A younger soul has not lived as many lifetimes and their soul is not as developed spiritually.

Even though old souls continue to learn here on Earth, their main purpose for being here is to enlighten those around them by giving them an opportunity for spiritual growth. (You can think of old souls as the older kids in school helping out the younger ones.) And these opportunities can appear in countless ways.

I was holding a small group reading once and a young girl named Cindy who was in her twenties wanted me to make a connection with her grandparents. So as I opened myself up, I could tell that her grandfather was ready to speak with her and Cindy became very excited when I told her this.

At first, he gave her several confirmations about the time they had shared together and affirmed that one of his favorite memories was when they used to decorate Easter eggs together.

Cindy said that confirmation touched her heart and she explained that they used to sit at the kitchen table together when she was a little girl, painting Easter eggs. She remembered when he would get out the food coloring and set up the bottles of bright colors in front of her. Boiling the eggs first, he would save the cracked ones for himself and give her the best ones. He described the cracked eggs as challenges that just needed his artistic touch. He would incorporate the most outrageous colors and those were her favorites. Her grandfather would then pick the winner (she always won), and he would place the egg he selected as the best on the mantle of the fireplace for all to see.

As Cindy was cheerfully recounting this memory, her grandmother started connecting with me and I could sense how very proud she was of this young girl. I relayed this to her. Tears started to well up in Cindy's eyes.

Her grandmother told Cindy that they knew how much Cindy had gone through in her life and how much she had helped everyone around her.

Cindy's mother and father were both alcoholics and had left both her and her younger brother behind with their grandparents when they were quite young. And even though they all lived together, the grandparents were much older and not in good health, so Cindy basically ran the household and had taken care of her younger brother since she was twelve. She was always a responsible girl and easily took charge of any situation, never complaining once. During the years when Cindy was growing up, her parents, who were still battling their demons, would check in occasionally only to find that as more time went by, Cindy was becoming older and wiser and attempting to assist them in overcoming their disease. Her grandparents were amazed by the maturity Cindy possessed when dealing with her parents, as well as very grateful to have her with them as their health started to deteriorate.

Life changed dramatically for Cindy when she was twenty-one and her brother had just turned eighteen as both of her grandparents passed in that same year. Her brother decided to join the army, and Cindy was left alone to start life anew. Cindy was now attending college and anxious to take a variety of classes as she wanted to explore all that this world had to offer.

Her grandmother then told Cindy that she was an old soul and there were reasons why certain events had taken place in their lives. She told Cindy that because of her efforts, not only was Cindy able to be present in her grandparents' time of need, but she also helped her parents to find the path to becoming well. She said that her experiences were also going to allow her to benefit others throughout her life. Cindy was so happy to hear this and thanked her grandparents for the messages. Cindy also said this confirmed why she had always felt older than she was.

———

Old souls have common traits and characteristics that define who they are. Below are only a few of many; see if you can identify with any of them.

Age—Have always felt older than their chronological age.

Nonjudgmental—Have a high degree of understanding of people's behavior and are very tolerant of others.

Ethical—Have an inherited compass of knowing right from wrong.

Confident—Have a knowing and reassurance in what they believe.

Selfless—Are concerned more for others than themselves, and are always giving.

Common sense—See things in this world with a wider and wiser perspective.

Easygoing—Are very likable and enjoy being with people.

Concerned—Feel deeply for people.

Not resentful—Not jealous of others' successes, talents, or achievements.

Educated by life—Are able to learn life lessons much easier than others.

Calm—Remain rational in harrowing situations.

Career—Have an occupation that rescues, or on their own try to help people.

Using the above list, the more that you are able to asso-ciate yourself with the examples, the older your soul prob-ably is.

I have been told that I am an old soul (and God knows I feel like I am one at times), but before you think that I am bragging, believe me, I am not. There are a countless number of people in this world with old souls (this could even be you), and of course some souls are older than others.

But old soul or young soul, we all are still in this life for one reason, and that reason is to learn from one another. Without each other and the many challenges people have here on this Earth, there would be no growth. As students, sometimes the lesson can be hard to learn; as a teacher, it can even be harder to give, but when all is said and done...the rewards are endless in comparison.

22: Higher Souls

A higher soul is different than an old soul as these souls are at a level even closer to God than most, which is something that every soul strives to be.

Higher souls are born into this world to become an intricate part of our lives. When you think of someone with a higher soul, you may imagine that these are people with higher stature in this life such as religious figureheads or people who have devoted their lives to God. Are these the people with higher souls? Perhaps, but it is more likely that it is the people you never thought about who are actually those possessing a higher soul.

These are the souls who are born into this world with extreme disabilities such as the handicapped, the mentally challenged, those with terminal illnesses, and numerous other challenges. These individuals are unable to take care of themselves or unable to survive in this world on their own, dependent upon the help of others. And these souls are here for one reason only … the betterment of our souls.

———

Not too long ago, I gave a reading to a woman named Beth who wanted me to make a connection with her passed loved ones. When she sat across from me, instantly a strong young male spirit came forward.

"There is a child with you," I said. "It is a boy and he has been running around you ever since you came in."

She gave me the biggest smile as her eyes began to well up with tears. "That is my dear sweet boy, Benjy!" she exclaimed.

"But there is more," I said. "I know Benjy is excited but he really won't keep still!" I always read between the lines to decipher why spirits speak or act as they do, and I knew there must be a reason for him to be jumping all around like this. "Did he have a problem with his legs?" I asked.

With that she looked up with eyebrows raised. "Yes!" Beth said. "He was in a wheelchair his entire life."

"I am so sorry," I said. "But it must be more than just that. He keeps pointing to his brain; I take it there was something wrong there as well?"

"Yes, yes! He was also very mentally challenged," Beth responded as she began to cry.

"Well, not anymore!" I said. "He is in perfect health now and very much wants you to know that."

Beth breathed a big sigh of relief as she wiped the tears from her cheeks.

Benjy was born with an extreme case of cerebral palsy, a disorder that affected his brain and nervous system functions. When Beth was first informed of this, she knew that she would be spending her entire life taking care of her son.

"Your son also wants you to know how much he loves you and how grateful he is for your taking such good care of him. He says he knows how difficult it was for you, but the pure love you both had and have for each other is the greatest gift of all," I told her.

Through sobs Beth replied, "I always told him he was my gift!"

With that, I too started to tear up as her son started to show me an image. "Benjy is showing me a red cross and places it with you. To me this means health. Are you dealing with a health issue or did you recently see a doctor?" I asked.

She replied, "Yes..."

And before she could continue with the rest of her sentence, her son jumped in.

"Wait," I said. "Your son is telling me to say that you are fine, no worries."

Beth told me that right after her son's passing, she found a lump in her breast. Of course, naturally upset about her son's passing, she wondered what else could go wrong. She prayed to her son to give her the strength to get through whatever it was and fortunately she'd found out that it was in fact not cancer.

She replied, "I knew he was helping me. I felt him with me!"

"Benjy wants you to know that he is with you every day and that it is now his turn to care for his mama!" I relayed to her.

This seemed to give her joy and I could tell from them both how proud they were of each other.

After her reading was completed, Beth told me that by raising a son who had such challenges, her life had changed in ways she never thought possible. It made her realize what was really important in life, and that was the love of her family and how much love she had inside to give. She said that even though most people saw her situation as tragic, for her it was the opposite and she thanked God every day for her wonderful boy.

———

In situations like this, some people wonder how a loving God can bestow such conditions on people, especially innocent children. There are some who even believe that the cause is Karma and that a person must have done something negative in a previous life to now be punished for it.

This is not the case at all.

These higher souls are graceful enough to dedicate an entire life here in this physical realm in order to provide those around them with the opportunity for soul growth through humility, passion, and love, which can be found within.

When you take a look at the bigger picture and know that this lifetime is really only a fleeting moment in your soul's eternal life, you will see how blessed someone is to be in the presence of such a higher soul, a soul who has chosen to help others with their life journey and their soul's growth.

23: End of the World

Throughout the history of humankind, there has always been speculation and warnings about the apocalypse and the end of the world, also known as "The Rapture."

It is believed that God is going to become so discouraged with everyone on Earth that one day he is going to open up the sky from the Heavens above and cause great destruction to the Earth. It is believed that graves will open and "the saved" will be taken to Heaven and the "not saved" will suffer an eternity in Hell.

My question is: Why would God have to be so dramatic?

Let's just say for argument's sake that God's mind works that way and he wanted to reward the good people by bringing them to Heaven and punish the bad people by sending them to Hell ... Why wouldn't he just snap his fingers and make it all happen? In less than the blink of an eye, the good could be in Heaven and the bad in Hell, if he so wanted. Why all the theatrics and fuss; why all the fire and brimstone?

And if you really think about it, since God is the creator of souls, why would he want to send any soul to Hell forever anyway? Why wouldn't he just decimate a person's soul to a nonexistent state? What would be the reason to keep a bad soul in Hell, just so God can say I told you so … forever and ever?

Really, would God be that petty and vengeful? No, he would not. But the scary part is that there are many people in this world who think that he would be. And why do they think this way?

Some religions teach that God is a vengeful God, and preach and predict that people are living in "the end time" and that the end of the world is going to occur in their lifetime. They say it now, they said it ten years ago, and they have been saying it for centuries and centuries. But why?

The reason religions do this is to put the fear of God into people. By using these "scare tactics," they convince people that they have all the answers concerning God and his Kingdom and if you follow and do what they tell you, you will be safe, saved—whatever you want to call it—and you will become one of those "chosen" to go to Heaven.

Just recently a man made headlines around the world by claiming that the world was about to end. Not only that, he said that he knew the exact date and time it was going to happen. This man had and still has many followers who quit their jobs, sold their houses, and basically gave up everything they had in order to help spread the word that the end times were near. The media had a field day with this as the time started ticking down, showing these believers standing in the streets, holding their signs, and warning people to give their lives to God in order to be saved. So the final moment arrived and the media focused on some of the followers who were standing in the crowd of people, and what happened? Nothing. The world did not end.

This man's followers just stood there with the public, slowly lowering their signs as people around them started laughing and mocking them. In all honesty, I felt sorry for them as they truly believed what they were doing was right and just wanted to help others. But unfortunately they were trying to do this by scaring people into believing in God.

One of the most amazing facts about this is that it was not the first time this man had predicted the end of the world; this was just one of many. He said that it was going to happen back in 1988; it did not. He then said it was going to happen in 1994; it did not. But even though he had been wrong every time, there were still people who believed him because they were afraid not to.

So when this last prediction did not come true, the media went to this man's house and asked him what had happened. Why didn't the world end? He replied that he had just miscalculated the time and that it was going to take place in another six months.

As you read this book, you can obviously see that this man was yet again wrong about the world coming to an end. But I will also bet if you were to look it up on the

internet, there will still be another date when he or someone else predicts the world is going to end.

An interesting note: because of his "followers," this
man is said to be worth over seventy million dollars. I
guess predicting the end of the world is also lucrative …

So is God ever really going to end the world?

I am not going to pretend to know what's on God's
mind, but logically, why would he?

Again, we live in this world in order for our souls to
learn from the conflicts we face and create for ourselves
in this life. And if we have not already done enough in our
past history, since time began, to make God want to end
the world by now, then I cannot imagine what it would
take for us to make him want to do so now.

The only way this world will be destroyed is by people,
not God … and when or how it ever happens is entirely up
to us.

24: Time on Earth

Consider how long summers are for a child.

I remember when I could not wait for that first day of summer vacation. It seemed like I had an eternity to be able to enjoy all that time off, playing outside all day and night with no homework and just being with friends. But eventually the day would come when it would all end and it was time to go back to school. It seemed as if summer just flew by and then it was time for another long school year.

But why is that? Why does it seem that time can go by so quickly on some days and slower on others?

The reason is because it has nothing to do with "time" at all, but rather your perspective and perception of what you are doing.

And believe it or not, there really is no such thing as "time."

Okay, I know, I know, you may be thinking that I am crazy, but let me explain.

Every second of your life, you are actually living in the present moment. You can think back about the past, what has happened in your life, and ponder the future, but life is taking place this moment and you are living in the now.

The concept of time is merely a manmade tool that helps people to organize, measure, and apply continuity to life.

So why then does time seem to go by so quickly at times and slowly at others?

The answer is simple ... perspective.

Anything you do in life that brings you pleasure or you concentrate on takes your mind off time. What is happening is that you are focusing on a certain aspect of your life and it is in this action that time seems to go by quickly. But the opposite also holds true as time seems to go by slower when you are concentrating on or experiencing something that is not bringing you pleasure. An example of this is how a work week can seem so long but a vacation week goes by in a moment, seemingly. In actuality, a moment is a moment and it is only your perception of what you are experiencing that makes it seem different.

This also holds true with perspective, as time seems to go by quicker the older one becomes. To a ten-year-old, five years would be half their lifespan and would seem like an eternity, whereas someone who is fifty years old would say that five years ago seems like only yesterday. If you were to ask any older person how fast time has gone by, I'd bet they will say they cannot believe how old they are and how quickly the years have passed.

And also because of perspective, time going forward always seems a lot longer than time that has already gone by. In other words, if you were to take today's date and think about this same time next year, it will seem to be a long time from now. But if you were to think about this time last year, it does not seem that long ago.

———

I once did a reading for a man named Randy. He was a little late for his session and apologized. I told him not to worry about it.

Right away I connected with an energetic young female spirit. This girl was so full of life and I could tell that she could not to wait to get started. Randy told me that he wanted to connect with his daughter, Amy, and I said she was already present with me.

"Your daughter is so excited; she is almost jumping up and down. In fact, she is jumping up and down," I told him enthusiastically.

"Well, she was a cheerleader in school," Randy replied.

"Apparently she still is!"

This placed a big grin on Randy's face, but I could tell by his voice that he was trying not to cry.

I continued. "To start off, I understand it was a very fast passing with Amy. Did she pass in an accident?"

With that, Randy broke down and started to weep. He replied that she did in fact pass in an accident a few years back.

"She is asking me to tell you that she did not see what was taking place and she felt no pain," I assured him.

Through his tears, Randy managed to say. "Oh God, I was hoping that was the case."

"It was and she wants you never to think that it wasn't," I affirmed. "She is mentioning something about coming home from school, was she in high school?"

"Yes, she was coming home from school. She was only seventeen."

"Amy wants you to know that she is alive and well and still as active as she ever was. She says that she never even sits down!"

This made Randy laugh and he responded, "That's how she always was her whole life."

I continued. "Well, Amy wants you to know that she still is and that she is proud of everything she accomplished in this life."

"We are so proud of everything she did," Randy agreed. "Amy was always on the go and had tireless energy. She joined all the clubs she could at school and participated in community service. Anytime we would tell her she needed to slow down, she would just smile and tell us she was doing what she loved. My girl always wanted to get the most out of every minute."

"And she is telling me she still does," I said. "Now for some reason, Amy is telling me to thank you for being late today. Why would she do that?" Her statement made me laugh.

Randy replied with another big grin, "I was hoping she was there because I could feel her with me! I started a foundation to honor her memory and hosted a 10K walk early this morning. This would be something Amy and I would do together in the past—God, that seems like only yesterday—so I thought holding a race would be a good way to honor my angel. But time being what it is, it slipped away and I had to rush in order to make this appointment!"

"Amy is telling me that the foundation means the world to her and she was right along with her father every step of the way! She also wants you to know that the 10K walk is going to help many people. But she laughingly says for you not to use that as an excuse for being late, as you are always late for everything!"

This brought a chuckle from Randy as he agreed with Amy and promised her that he would try not to let time get away from him.

———

In conclusion, there is really no such thing as time. It is just the memories of the life you have lived, the present moment you are now experiencing, and the thoughts you have about the future.

Keep in mind, it is never the amount of time that you have that matters in this life—but how you spend it that really counts.

25: Fulfilling & Happy Life

There is no question that life can be challenging ... but guess what? It is for everyone, and this is why we are all here in the first place as our souls learn and grow from each obstacle we face in this life.

But with so many challenges in this world, is it really possible to find happiness?

The good news: Yes, of course it is!

As a medium, not only do I connect people with their loved ones in spirit, but I too share in the lessons learned during our sessions. It has given me a greater appreciation for life and how to live it. I would like to share some of these lessons with you.

Even though this world is a classroom, God does want us to enjoy ourselves while we are here. To be happy in this life, you first need to understand where happiness truly comes from and then take the proper steps to achieve it.

SURVIVING

To begin, one of the main reasons that so many people are unhappy in this world is that they are concentrating so much on just "surviving" in it that they are not taking the time for "living" in it. By that I mean recognizing and enjoying the positive things that are actually already all around us.

One of the most common reasons people are unhappy in this life is that they are not satisfied with their job, career, work—however you refer to what you do in order to make a living.

It goes without saying that most adults have to work to be able to exist in this world and/or to take care of their family. But due to any number of reasons, many people end up in a job that they do not like. These people struggle to get through the work week just to get to the weekend or their days off. How many times have you heard a person say or have even said to yourself, "I just want to get through the day," or "I cannot wait until this week is over"? With this logic, people with this attitude are actually only enjoying the weekends, which is two days out of the week, eight days a month, 104 days a year, and so on. And then, of course, what always happens? The weekend or time off goes by in the blink of an eye and then the whole cycle starts all over again. If you think about it, that amount of time is really a small segment of life for someone to be happy and a very large amount of life for someone not to be happy.

Why is it that so many people stay at a job where they are miserable in the first place? Now if you were to say that they do this in order to survive and/or to take care of their family, you'd have a pretty good reason … but still not the main reason. The key to why people work someplace where they are not happy is because it is human nature that the "known" is more comfortable than the "unknown," and change can have an unknown factor to it.

This is the reason so many people would rather stay unhappy in a current situation rather than take a chance with a future one … even if this move could possibly bring more happiness into their lives. I find that when most people (and I will include myself) go after their dreams, they discover they have a happier life, even if this action brings on more struggle than before, as it is better to do something hard in this life that you enjoy rather than do something easy that you do not enjoy.

I know, I know, you may say that it would take a lot of effort on your part to change your life and you know what, you would be right. Anything you really want is going to take exertion and energy on your part, but that is when life is the most rewarding and where you will find the most happiness.

The richest people will tell you that if you find a job that you love, you never will work a day in your life. And when I say the richest people, I do not necessarily mean monetarily.

And the good news is that you do not have to have that dream job today in order to be happy!

Once you get the courage to start taking the steps necessary to change your life in this way, you will instantly possess a new outlook, one you have never had before.

And the courage necessary could be as little as just sitting down by yourself and writing a list of anything and everything you would like to do. You will be surprised by how just the action of writing something down can set the wheels in motion for these dreams to actually become a reality. And it does not matter how big or how crazy the concepts you write down may seem to you or to anyone else for that matter, the greater the goal you strive for the greater the result you will receive!

I have done this myself in the past, and let me tell you I too had my doubts. One of the things on my list was to write a book. At that time, anyone who knew me would have laughed that item right off my list because I was definitely not the author type and for me to be able to put paragraphs together to form some cohesive message would had been a miracle from up above. I didn't care and I put it on my list anyway.

Today, besides being a medium, I am a bestselling author, and my books have been published in many countries around the world. I am not bragging (though I do throw this out at those who have doubted me from time to time), but I am making a point. If creating a list works for me, it can work for you too!

———

I know you would love to just go to the job you have today and say "I quit!" And even though that may bring you a "moment" of happiness, it would last only as long as it took you to walk out the door and start thinking about how you were going to start paying your bills. So let's not quit just yet…

After you compose your list, keep your newfound momentum going by planning what it is going to take in order for you to achieve your dream job.

- Are you going to need to take a course or class?
- Do you need to speak with someone who is already in the same field to get some advice?
- Can you find out more about it on the Internet?
- Is it a matter of starting to save in order to buy something you may need for it?
- Is it just a matter of setting aside some time in your life to begin pursuing it?

These are just a few questions to get you thinking, but you are the one who knows what you want to do, so take the necessary action to make it happen!

Just like the list you made above, make another one comprised of the steps you can take to start down the path to your dream job!

Just by making these lists you are putting out positive energy, and it is a universal fact that positive brings positive.

You may be thinking to yourself, this is too easy and nothing like that will work. You would be wrong because it is that simple. Everything you do in life begins with an idea, and that idea turns into passion, and that passion is what transforms your dreams into reality!

So by your continuing to concentrate on taking the next steps, even the job you have today will not seem as difficult or miserable as it did before, because you are now on your path to a happier tomorrow!

MONEY & THINGS

People often think that the more things they own in this life, the happier they will be. This is a really huge misconception.

First, of course, there are certain basic things that you need in life in order to survive, such as food, water, and shelter. Next come the items that help to make this life more convenient, such as items you use for transportation, entertainment, and so on. Certainly these things can bring happiness as they make life more comfortable, easier, and more pleasurable.

But if you go beyond the items that are necessities for survival or comfort, what are you left with? Items that will usually bring only a temporary feeling of pleasure, something that does not last.

Living in this physical world, people attach emotions to physical objects that they possess as it is human nature to do so. When something new comes into one's life, there is usually a sense of enthusiasm as well as excitement. These positive emotions are created because of the perception of what these items will mean to one's everyday existence. At the time, these feelings are real and concrete, but the only problem is, they can and eventually will change.

How many times have you seen a child who could not wait to receive a special toy that they wanted for Christmas? This toy meant so much to them that their whole life revolved around having it. For weeks leading up to Christmas, that was all they talked about. So on Christmas day when they opened the box and saw the toy that they wanted so desperately, it brought them so much joy and excitement that they could not stop jumping up and down.

But what always happens?

After the Christmas tree is taken down and the toy has been played with a few times, the child loses interest in it and the toy ends up just sitting in the corner of the room or on a shelf, never to be touched again. The wonderful item that once brought the child so much pleasure and excitement no longer does. I know many of you are nodding your heads up and down in agreement as you have experienced this phenomenon with a child yourself. That is just the way kids are—but do not think you are getting off that easy, adults act the same way too...

Let's use an example of a big boy's toy, like a car for instance. Many people will go out and buy a new car that places a financial burden on them, one that is usually not needed. But the excitement of having a stylish new car and being able to show it off to family and friends far outweighs the negatives like having the larger monthly payments that come with it... that is, at the time of the purchase anyway. So these people happily buy the car, feeling good about their purchase, and show it off to their family and friends. The new car smell, the leather seats, and all the new electronic gadgets that go with it are proudly displayed. By doing so, the owners will usually receive lots of compliments and congratulations on their new purchase, which also makes them feel great and look forward to the positive accolades on the car still to come.

But (and you know there is a "but") then what always happens?

After a few weeks go by and, when everyone has seen the new car, the compliments and congratulations slow down and eventually come to an end. But what does not come to an end are the monthly payments on the car. And with that, all of a sudden the same emotion the owners once had for this brand new car starts to fade away and in very little time not only does the car become just a car, it now has negative feelings associated with it because of the monthly payments that are attached.

The love affair with the car ends … so sad.

So you see that the positive emotions that were once associated with the car have been replaced by the negative emotions of dread and worry over having to pay for the car.

But let's say you were rich and could buy any car that you wanted and not have to worry about car payments, certainly then you would be happy … right?

Not necessarily.

Most people believe that money can "buy" happiness. They feel if someone is able to buy anything they want and any amount they want of it, then certainly happiness can be bought! But if you think about it, if that were really the case, then why are so many rich people miserable?

One of the biggest fallacies people have is that the bigger the house and the more cars someone has, the more happiness these things will bring. Can these inanimate objects bring a person more comfort? Certainly, but there is a big difference between "comfort" and "happiness" … never mistake the two.

The one thing I can tell you that money can in fact buy is "boredom." That's right, I said it—boredom!

I have spoken with many wealthy people in this world and some of these people were unhappy because they were just plain and simply bored! Having everything at your fingertips does not automatically make a person understand their purpose in life—and without purpose, there is no chance for happiness. I remember a famous actress once telling me that she was very unhappy. This woman had everything going for her, fame, fortune; all that most people think would bring joy. So I asked her why she was so distressed and she replied, "Because how many television sets or houses can I buy?"

Now I know you may be thinking to yourself: if only you could have such a problem! But that really is the point. It does not matter what you have or what you do not have, it is what you strive for that will bring you bliss.

This is why those who are rich and contribute their time and fortunes to help others in need are the ones who are truly the happiest of the wealthy, not because of the things they own or the money they have. And this is why you too can find joy with any amount of money you may have.

Do not get me wrong, there can be items a person can have that will, in fact, make them happy forever, these being the items that have emotions and memories attached to them. It could be a gift that someone has given to another person or an item someone has inherited from a passed love one. It could also be what someone made for the one they love. It does not matter if the item is large or small, valuable or worthless, what makes this item valuable is not the actual object itself, but the emotion that is connected to it, feelings that never go away.

This is called "sentimental value" and it can make any item the most precious and priceless belonging one can ever own.

PERSPECTIVE

What can also bring happiness in your life is understanding your own viewpoint on life itself.

I am sure you are familiar with the phrase, "You can look at the glass as half empty or half full." And even though this is a simple statement, it is one of the most exact and precise concepts that can be used to define a person's outlook on life and who they truly are.

Perspective is your personal viewpoint on everything and how you judge its relative importance—it is basically how you see the world!

I touched earlier in this book on how we all have our own perspective on life that forms our opinions on what we do and who we are. But perspective will also form thoughts and feelings in you, thereby guiding you on every aspect of your life.

People who live with the attitude that "things are good, but they could be worse," are going to be much happier in life than those with the attitude that "things are good, but they could be better." You see, in both examples things are "good" (not great), but it is how you perceive "good" that matters!

An example of this is when I once had a phone client named Nate who worked on Wall Street and I would connect him with his family and friends in spirit. This man was worth about four million dollars and he always complained to me during our conversations that he was not happy because he felt that he was not doing as well as others he knew. I would say to Nate that he was already very well off and that it was okay to strive for success, but it was even more important to enjoy what he already had. This would always go in one ear and out the other, as he would just continue to complain. When the market crashed a few years ago, unfortunately Nate did lose about half of his money, bringing his net worth down from four million dollars to about two million dollars, and he was devastated! In talking with him, I tried to give Nate some perspective by helping him realize that even though he'd lost a great deal of money, he still had a great deal of money. This did not matter to Nate; through self-blinders, all he could see was what he had lost and not what he still had: great health and a great deal of money, and still he was not happy.

This is an example of when someone is a victim of their own thinking. When a person is not happy with what they have, and unhappy with what they do not have, consequently, they are only self-sabotaging their own happiness.

Speaking of the stock market, actor Kevin Bacon and his wife Kyra Sedgwick also went through the same ordeal as in the above example with Nate. During the same crash of the market, they too lost millions of dollars, and even though I am sure at first they may have wanted to put their fists through the wall (and maybe they even did), they both dusted themselves off and said that it was no big deal. And why did they have such a great attitude? Because Kevin said it was only money and he did not lose what was actually the most important part of his life … his family.

Again, the identical circumstance was happening to two different people, both having a different perspective, making one person still happy and the other miserable. In both cases, it was up to them to determine how they felt about their situation through their perspective.

But it is certainly all right if you initially react in a negative way when there is a negative occurrence; again, that is being human. But right after the "reaction" takes place, it is important to take "action" and realize the positive and important parts of your life.

The good news is that you can do this with anything in your life!

All you need to do is to remember what is good in your life, even if it is just one aspect, and build from there!

You are the architect of your own life—so you might as well construct the best one possible!

APPRECIATION

The last action I want to suggest to you in order for you to find happiness in your life is something you can do as soon as you close this book.

That is to take a moment, close your eyes, and appreciate everything that you already have.

People have a tendency to become complacent with the many parts of their lives that surround them—be it health, home, family, or friends, anything that becomes what is considered to be the "norm" in someone's everyday existence starts being taken for granted, thereby not appreciated. As another saying goes, "You never know what you have until it is gone." That also is a powerful quote as it usually takes a loss before we really appreciate what we once possessed.

This is why it is important for "re-appreciation" (another word I just coined, meaning to learn to appreciate something again) of what you have.

When you are having a bad day, and who doesn't, take just a moment to go outside and look around you. God has given us such beauty in this world through nature that all you need to do is notice it! You may be thinking to yourself that you see it all the time! But I am not talking about checking the weather; I'm talking about actually appreciating the weather! Whether it is going to look at birds, flowers, trees, the sky, sunrise, sunset, clouds, moon, animals, attractive people (oops ... that last one just slipped out), whatever it might be, just spend a moment and take it all in. It is God's "quick fix" that can turn any negative moment into a positive one instantly!

Don't believe ... just try it!

Another item people take for granted that is one of the most important is "health."

If you think about it, no matter if you have a bad job, have only a few possessions, have little to no money, or even cars that do not work, if you have your health, you have everything already as health is the mechanics of our physical body that allows us to do what we do and create what we hope to make in this world.

Being healthy allows you to accomplish anything you want in this life, but you need the fortitude to do so. I find it amazing how many people take the greatest gift one could have for granted—being healthy—while those who are unhealthy would give any amount of money to be able to have it.

I was watching a reality show once where one of the participating contestants was missing a leg. This person never griped about it and never felt she was handicapped; in fact, she wanted to be treated like everyone else. The goal of this show was to win a million dollars, and of course all of the contestants wanted to win it. And why not? This is what they were playing for and a million dollars could change anyone's life.

But I would bet that if the person who was missing a leg were to have won the million dollars, this person would have traded the million dollars in a heartbeat for two healthy legs instead of one, a gift all the other contestants already had. So if you think about it, all of the other contestants already had a possession that was worth more than a million dollars—their health—already making them the "winners."

However, being unhealthy does not give someone a free pass to not be happy, as perspective still applies.

Whatever may be wrong with you, there is always someone else out there who is worse off. As in the example above with the woman missing one of her legs, no matter how challenging it is for her to get around in life, it would be even more difficult if she was missing both of her legs.

So it does not matter if you do have a physical handicap, even though life may be more of a struggle for you, as long as your mind is sharp and you have a positive outlook on life, anything is possible, especially happiness.

And the most important factor that people sometimes take for granted is … a loved one.

I know you may be thinking to yourself, "not me!" But let me ask you, is there someone who is or has been a part of your life that you may not have spoken to in a while?

The reason I am bringing this up is that I speak from experience. In my line of work, every single day I hear people telling me that they wished they had spoken to or told loved ones how they felt about them before they passed. Most people habitually put off getting in touch with others, thinking they will do it tomorrow. The only problem with that is … many people do not have a "tomorrow."

If you think about it, everything you do in life that brings happiness is usually connected with sharing thoughts and feelings with someone else.

If I were to ask you what are some of the happiest times you have experienced, what would come to mind? Take a moment and think about this.

Did you think of …

- The birth of a child?
- A certain holiday?
- A vacation you took?
- A wedding perhaps?
- A child's first step?

No matter what the thought was that just brought a smile to your face, I would bet you one thing … it also involved another person being with you!

Whether it is a lover, family, friend, neighbor, or even just someone you say hello to at a store, interaction between people is how you educate yourself in life, and give your soul growth, making you who you are and thereby bringing happiness into your life.

Having someone to share your life with and appreciating them is the greatest source of joy anyone can have in this life, and this world is too big with too many people in it for you not to be happy.

IN CONCLUSION

Happiness in life comes not from the outside, but is created from within. You do not have to have money or physical objects in order to obtain happiness. Most people will never have enormous amounts of money or fame and that is why God designed happiness to be found in the simpler aspects of the everyday, in people that you love, not in having things.

If people wait until they achieve possessions, a great accomplishment, or become famous before they can ever be happy in life, then they will probably not be happy for long. It is actually the "wanting" that keeps people moving forward in this life, and this is good as the more you forge ahead, the more your spirit learns and grows.

The important thing is not to wait until you reach your dream or achieve a goal before becoming happy, but to appreciate and enjoy everything that you already have and to share your life with others.

Because your life "is the journey" and it is up to YOU to make it a happy and fulfilling one…

PART 4
LIGHTER SIDE OF THE OTHER SIDE

When I am giving a reading, the individual receiving the messages can experience many emotions. From love, understanding, hope, to even relief, feelings become tangible as the loved ones in spirit try to comfort and console through the communication they convey.

But just as with anyone else, a spirit can have a sense of humor and will also use this emotion as a confirmation and to help their loved one with the healing process...

26: Spiritual Antidotes

PASS THE MAYONNAISE

Recently I was giving a reading to a woman who wanted to hear from her husband in spirit. As I began the reading, her husband approached me to anxiously start communicating with his wife, but I could tell there also was a mother figure in spirit with him wanting to join the conversation as well. So I concentrated on speaking with him first and he was able to relay wonderful messages to his wife. But as I continued conversing with him, the mother figure in spirit kept trying to interrupt the conversation and I could tell that he was actually becoming a bit frustrated with her. Come to find out, it was the wife's mother, his mother-in-law, and she then took over. I could tell that this made the husband in spirit more anxious as he knew his mother-in-law was a talker! She was happy to connect with her daughter and seemed to not want to stop talking. Finally, when I connected back with him, he told me to say to his wife "mayonnaise." I thought to myself, what an unusual message to give to someone, and wondered if he or she had a thing for mayonnaise and this was some sort of strange confirmation. But like I always do, I said what I heard and told this woman that her husband wanted me to say mayonnaise. With that she became excited and asked me if he was talking about May May? I laughed and asked, what is a May May? She told me that her mother in spirit is named May May and that her husband used to call her mayonnaise when she got on his nerves. So with that we all saw the humor in that her husband was getting back at his mother-in-law for butting into the reading!

MOWING THE PATH TO HEAVEN

Speaking with a husband in spirit, I was telling his wife over the phone details about his passing over. He kept giving me the sensation that something struck his head and when I told her this, she confirmed that it had. He then visually gave me an image that he was cutting grass and when I said this to her, she began to cry. She told me that he had been mowing the lawn and while he was under a tree, a branch fell and struck him in his head and her husband died instantly. To bring a smile to his loving wife's face her husband cracked a joke and said, "Talk about timing!" He continued with the story and described his passing to us both. Her husband explained that he was just enjoying a beautiful day outside and decided to cut the grass. As he was doing so, he felt something hit his head. He said it knocked him to the ground but that he shook it off and was surprised that he did not feel any pain. So as her husband stood back up on his feet he suddenly realized that there were people in his yard, but not just any people, it was his relatives and friends … people who had passed. He shook his head again, trying to clear it, thinking he might have been more hurt than he realized. He thought perhaps he might have received a concussion from being hit on the head and he might be hallucinating. They were all still standing there smiling at him and then he realized that he was not seeing things at all and said to himself, "Oh F#@%." At that, he said, all of his relatives started to laugh … as well as myself and his wife.

BATHROOM HUMOR

In lectures that Kathy and I hold, I usually will tell the audience members that their loved ones in spirit can be with them anywhere and everywhere that they go, but not to worry, they won't follow them into the bathroom. Well, with one reading that I was giving, I was speaking with a man whose partner had passed away from a long illness. They both loved each other very much and this man took care of his dying partner day in and day out up until the day he passed into spirit. As I was giving this man his partner's messages of love and confirmations, all of a sudden this spirit wanted me to tell his mate that he watched him in the bathroom. Again, I do have my own reactions to what spirits will want me to tell someone and this message started to make me laugh, but I always go along with the flow. So I informed this man that his partner wanted him to know that he was with him in the bathroom. When this man heard the message, he too burst into laughter as well as wept tears of joy. He said that before his partner had passed, he told this man who was receiving the reading that even after he passed, he would always be with him no matter where, even in the bathroom! Confirmations from a loved one can come in so many ways…

SIZE DOES MATTER

A woman came to me for a reading, wanting me to do something that I do not normally do, and that is for me to not only connect with a husband, but with two of them in spirit. I find requests like this quite interesting as I never know where the conversation is going to lead. So I opened myself up and first I felt one husband starting to make the connection with me, and then right beside him also stood her other husband, both ready to talk! When I connect with a spirit, I can always tell what kind of person/spirit they are by being able to sense their personality. So with her two husbands, I knew that one was more of a no-nonsense kind of guy (her first husband), whereas the other one had a lighter and funnier personality (her second husband). The one thing she wanted to know was if they knew each other in spirit and how they got along. The first husband said that of course they knew each other and that her "husband number two," as he put it, was driving him crazy with his bad jokes. So her second husband responded by saying that husband number one was just mad at him, not only because he was the better lover between the two, but because he had the bigger "wing." We all got the joke.

CHECKING OUT SPIRITS

A woman came to me who had been very concerned about what her husband in spirit would think of what she had started to do again, and that was dating. This is not an unusual question from people in such situations as there can be many mixed emotions and confusion when dealing with this decision. On the one hand, some people want to continue on with their lives, especially if they are younger, and find someone else to love. But on the other hand, they still continue to love their spouse in spirit and by doing so naturally feel guilty for wanting to find another love here. Any spouse in spirit will "usually" understand someone wanting to do this and will encourage and even help their loved one here in finding another love, as they know that this person will always love them and they want their spouse to be happy.

So when this woman asked her husband what his feelings were about this situation, his reply made me laugh. He said to his wife that it was certainly all right for her to go out and look for another guy because he told her not to forget that there are girls in Heaven too! She laughed at this and said that he always had a "wandering eye." And he still does.

NOT A SAINT

At a demonstration, I connected to a son in spirit who was giving me messages for his mother and sister who were in the audience. I could tell that he was full of life and that he always did things his way. He gave his family many confirmations, including that he knew his sister was about to get married and he looked forward to attending the ceremony. He also relayed to the audience and his family how amazed and surprised he was by his mother getting a tattoo! With that, his mother lifted her shirt sleeve to reveal a tattoo. The audience laughed as well with that bit of news. All of this information brought tears of joy to their eyes as they knew that he was not only still alive, but still himself. What he then said jokingly made everyone in the crowd laugh as well as me and his family. He said that even though he was in Heaven, he was still acting wild and was "not a saint" and told them he should know—he's actually met some real saints!

NO SCORE!

I remember speaking with a woman who wanted me to connect with her husband. We sat down and I opened myself up for him to come. I usually am always able to communicate with whomever the person is looking to speak with, but for some reason her grandmother was the one who spoke first. So after giving her messages from her grandmother, I still did not feel her husband with me, but rather now it was her grandfather. So as I was speaking with him, relaying his messages to her, I finally felt her husband making a connection with me as well. I thought to myself that it was kind of strange that her husband was not the first one to speak, but I can only do what the spirits want to do. So once I made my connection with her husband, he laughed and told his wife that he was sorry for being late. She smiled and told him that she was not surprised. I then went on from there and started conveying to her messages that brought much comfort to her. But while all of this was going on, I could tell that he was distracted. When I told his wife what was taking place, she too became curious as to what he was doing. I asked him if something was diverting his attention and he held up a basketball. When I told his wife that he was holding up a basketball, she started laughing and knew exactly what was going on. At the time of the reading, his favorite basketball team was playing in a playoff and she wondered if he would be able to see the game! He chuckled at this and told her that she was correct, but the only reason he was watching the game was as a confirmation for her. She continued laughing and called him a liar and then we also both knew that was the reason he was late for her reading! She thanked her grandparents for covering for him. He also added that one of the best parts of Heaven was that they can be courtside at any game and not know what the outcome will be!

ASH ME LATER

In a small group where I was giving a reading, a young woman in attendance wanted to receive messages from her father. After I connected and received several communications from him, I could tell that he was a lighthearted soul who loved his family very much. At one point her father started discussing his remains and this made his daughter sit up in her chair. He said that his family cremated him and she agreed this was true and was the reason why she was participating in the group reading. She said that once the cremation took place, her family did not know what to do with their father's ashes and wanted to know what he wished them to do. Jokingly, he told his daughter just to put them in a peppermill as this would make it easier for her to share them with everyone. Everyone started laughing at this and I could tell this spirit enjoyed the reaction and continued speaking. He then told his daughter that it honestly did not matter to him what she did with the ashes because it wasn't even him anyway, the cremators accidently gave her the ashes of a dog. She gasped at this, thinking he was serious, and I told her that her father was laughing and I could tell that he was only joking. We all laughed even harder with that comment.

BRAGGING RIGHTS

Once I was giving a radio interview and taking callers. Everything was going great, with many good calls, and the hosts were excited that everyone was having such a great time. So while this was taking place, a man called, wanting me to connect with his mother. As I proceeded, his mother did in fact make a connection with me and I could tell she had a lot to say. Many times during a reading like this, the spirit I am speaking with may say something about themselves, but since they have only a minute or two with me and their loved one on the radio, they will usually talk about and give advice to the person who has asked for the reading. The unusual thing about this caller's mother was that she seemed to only want to talk about herself. I told him that she wanted him to know what a good person she was and how much she loved her family. The caller's mother then started to list some her accomplishments, which seemed a bit odd to me, but I delivered the messages. The man on the phone would chime in from time to time with a "yes, mom" and "okay, mom" and this even started to make the radio hosts laugh. As we continued, I told the caller that his mother said that she hoped this helped. I thought to myself, how is bragging on yourself going to assist your son? Once the reading was over the radio hosts asked the caller what he thought. The man could not have been happier. This caller's mother's funeral was actually taking place that morning and he was to deliver the eulogy. He was nervous and unsure as to what to say, so his wonderful mother was more than happy to help out!

27: In Closing

I recognize how hard it is to lose someone who has been an essential part of your life, but by knowing you have not lost them and that they continue and will continue to always be a part of your life, I hope you find the strength you need to keep moving forward and live the fulfilled life you are meant to have.

My goal and my hope in writing this book has been to shed light on what this life is about, what awaits you in the next, what not to be afraid of, and most of all, to help bring you closer to those you love in spirit.

I also wanted you to have an insight into what a medium really is and an inside glimpse of what my life has been like (so far) while being a medium.

People often call what I have a gift, and I guess in some ways, they are right. I do feel very fortunate knowing what I know and being able to share it with others as well as guiding people in discovering their own truths in their lives.

Some of my friends will tease me on occasion about being a medium. They say that because I have written books and have been on television all over the world that I must have a big head. I know they are only joking because anyone who really knows me recognizes that what I do comes from the heart, never from ego. And besides, even if I wanted to have a big head, the other side (and Kathy) would not even allow it ...

Just recently I was with Kathy and our friend Gina at one of our favorite places to eat, The Virginia Diner. This is a diner in Wakefield, Virginia, that opened back in the 1920s, a place we have frequented since we were children. They are famous for their ham biscuits and peanut pie, and just good food all around.

While we were enjoying our meal, several people came to us stating they have seen us on television and wanted us to know how much they enjoyed our work. This is always encouraging to hear and we told them how much we both appreciated the kind words. Once they left, we kidded with Gina, laughingly saying that it just comes with the territory of being "big famous celebrities."

But as we continued our meal, we noticed another person who just kept staring at us at a table from afar, and we figured that she too knew who we were. As soon as we finished, this young woman approached our table and said that she had seen the other people approach us and asked if it was okay if her friend took a picture of us together. I told her that I would be happy to let her do that, and as I got up and stood beside her preparing for the picture, she said to me that she enjoyed all of my films.

At that moment, my eyes slowly closed and I asked her, who do you think I am … knowing what the answer would be …

She replied excitedly, "The guy from the Harry Potter movies, Alan Rickman!"

I just shook my head and lowered it in disbelief as her friend snapped the picture.

Even with everything I have done, I am still being mistaken for the actor Alan Rickman. This is just another way Heaven is keeping me grounded, I guess …

But does having this gift of mediumship actually make me any more special than anyone else here in Heaven's eyes?

Not hardly …

Everyone in this world who has God in their heart, holds no prejudice against others, and loves his fellow man is just as special in Heaven's eye … of this, I am sure.

———

The bottom line is that this life is a lesson and what you learn from it is totally up to you. But remember, it is not "how" you learn, but "what" you learn that counts, and by keeping that thought in your mind, life can be pretty simple. Once you get past all the hustle and bustle of the world, all the drama and challenges, the one and only thing you can truly take back with you to God when you return to spirit is love … the single most important gift God has given us all.

———

So here I continue on my own life's path being a medium. I truly have enjoyed those of you who I have met so far and look forward to meeting many more of you (and your loved ones in spirit) somewhere down the road ...

TO WRITE TO THE AUTHOR

If you wish to contact the author or would like more information about this book, please write to the author in care of Llewellyn Worldwide Ltd. and we will forward your request. Both the author and publisher appreciate hearing from you and learning of your enjoyment of this book and how it has helped you. Llewellyn Worldwide Ltd. cannot guarantee that every letter written to the author can be answered, but all will be forwarded. Please write to:

Patrick Mathews
℅ Llewellyn Worldwide
2143 Wooddale Drive
Woodbury, MN 55125-2989

Please enclose a self-addressed stamped envelope for reply, or $1.00 to cover costs. If outside the U.S.A., enclose an international postal reply coupon.

For more information on Patrick Mathews visit his web site at : www.PatrickMathews.com.